Joseph Foster

Record of the Soldiers, Sailors and Marines Who Served the United States of America

in the war of the rebellion and previous wars; buried in the city of

Portsmouth, N.H. and the neighboring towns of Greenland, Newcastle,

Newington and Rye. May 30, 18

Joseph Foster

Record of the Soldiers, Sailors and Marines Who Served the United States of America
in the war of the rebellion and previous wars; buried in the city of Portsmouth, N.H. and the neighboring towns of Greenland, Newcastle, Newington and Rye. May 30, 18

ISBN/EAN: 9783337318222

Printed in Europe, USA, Canada, Australia, Japan

Cover: Foto ©ninafisch / pixelio.de

More available books at **www.hansebooks.com**

RECORD

OF THE

SOLDIERS, SAILORS AND MARINES

WHO SERVED THE

UNITED STATES OF AMERICA

IN THE

WAR OF THE REBELLION

AND PREVIOUS WARS:

BURIED IN THE CITY OF PORTSMOUTH, N. H.

AND THE NEIGHBORING TOWNS OF

GREENLAND, NEWCASTLE, NEWINGTON AND RYE.

MAY 30, 1893.

PREPARED FOR

STORER POST, NO. 1,

DEPARTMENT OF NEW HAMPSHIRE,

GRAND ARMY OF THE REPUBLIC,

PORTSMOUTH, N. H.

BY

JOSEPH FOSTER,

Paymaster, U. S. Navy.

PORTSMOUTH, N. H.

PRINTED AT THE OFFICE OF THE PORTSMOUTH JOURNAL.

1893.

A SOLDIER'S GRAVE.

MARIAN DOUGLAS.

Glad robins singing in the boughs,
  Low murmur of the bees,
A hill-side burying ground closed round
  With wilding apple-trees:
The snowy flowers drift softly down
  Upon the quiet graves,
And in the south wind over one,
  A small flag gently waves.

Those floating colors make for me
  That grassy mound a shrine.
What though the one who sleeps beneath
  Knew naught of me or mine?
Yet that brave life, quenched long ago,
  Seems of my own a part;
For he who dies for freedom, lives
  In every freeman's heart.

Harper's Bazar, May 28, 1892.

OUR SOLDIERS AND SAILORS.

"To New Hampshire men the whole nation is a sepulchre, for their blood has watered the soil of every state but their own, and their dust is mouldering by every great river and in every mountain pass from Maine to Georgia—from the Charles to the Rio Grande and the Red River of the North. They died before Warren at Bunker Hill, before Washington at Yorktown, under the eye of Jackson at New Orleans; they were thrown in their hammock-shroud from the bloody deck of Paul Jones, and Lawrence, and Decatur, and Farragut: they marched with Sherman, they charged with Sheridan, they conquered with Thomas, they fought it out on his own line with Grant. But no soldier of my native state ever fell on his own soil, or was buried in his dear native earth, unless the restless ocean cast his body on its narrow sea coast, or the love and care of parent, or brother, or child, restored to their sorrow and pride the corpse that had fallen a thousand miles from home."

Hon. F. B. Sanborn, of Concord, Mass.,
in the Massachusetts Legislature, March 14, 1889

THE GRAVES WE DECORATE.

The Regiments are Infantry unless otherwise stated.
A * indicates that a stone has not yet been erected.

Name.	*Service.*	*Rank or Ship.*	*Died.*	*Age.*	*Cemetery.*	*Part.*
Abbott, George Clark	U S Navy	Boatswain	14 Aug 1866	29	H Grove	East
Abbott, Samuel P	13th N H	Priv Co K	9 Nov 1880	44	Cotton's	Northwest
Adams, Charles F	"	Serg Co E	28 Apr 1871	43	H Grove	East
Adams, Horace H	10th N H	Corp Co G	10 Nov 1864	20	"	"
Adams, John Frank	27th Maine	Priv Co G	4 Dec 1874	32	"	Center
Adams, Patrick	6th N H	Priv Co H	15 Oct 1892	59	St Mary's	East*
Adams, William C	War 1812	....	14 Dec 1868	82	Newington	Center*
Amazeen, Joseph	U S R M	Captain	20 Apr 1880	67	H Grove	"
Anderson, James F	16th N H	Priv Co K	28 Jun 1876	75	"	Northwest
Anderson, James F	....	....	13 Mar 1865	20	"	"
Anderson, John	Mex War	....	20 Aug 1847	34	"	"
Atchison, George C	U S Navy	....	26 Apr 1864	55	North	West
Austin, Benj M	....	....	13 Apr 1883	45	H Grove	South
Ayers, James S	10th N H	Corp Co G	28 Jun 1868	...	"	South-west
Bailey, George F	6 I & 1 C Mass	Pr F & Cp D	19 Mar 1869	34	"	North-east
Bailey, William	U S Navy	....	27 Jun 1864	22	"	North-west
Banks, John S	....	....	4 Sep 1882	33	"	North
Banks, Orrin	War 1812.	....	....	...	"	" *
Barnes, William A	U S Navy	Kearsarge	12 Feb 1884	40	St Mary's	South-west
Barr, Ferdinand	13th N H	Priv Co K	18 Jul 1871	31	H Grove	East
Barry, William H	1st N H H Art	Priv Co A	26 Jan 1867	20	Newington	Center
Barsantee, Alphonzo	2nd Mass Bat	Priv	11 Jun 1866	33	H Grove	"
Barsantee, John B	War 1812	Let of Mar	1 Sep 1875	76	"	"
Bartow, Theodore B	U S Navy	Chaplain	17 May 1869	62	"	"
Bates, Patrick	U S M C	Priv	....	...	St Mary's	South-east
Bates, Robert	"	Sergeant	11 Jul 1892	60	Propr's	North—S W*
Baxter, George D	1st N Y Art	Priv Co G	9 Aug 1888	76	"	South—S
Beal, Freeman G	U S Navy	Pay Clerk	 1881	53	H Grove	North-east
Bennett, Abner B	U S Army	Surgeon	24 Jul 1867	44	Propr's	North—S E
Benson, Charles A	U S Navy	Colorado	16 Jul 1890	60	"	South—S*
Berry, Albert C	4th N H	1 Serg Co B	13 Jul 1873	33	H Grove	West
Bickford, Andrew	Mex War	Priv C 9 U S	3 Apr 1871	68	Newington	Center
Binch, David	9th N H	Priv Co C	6 Sept 1863	35	Propr's	South—N*
Bishop, Henry J	U S M C	Captain	22 Dec 1884	46	"	South—N W
Black, William	U S Navy	Boatswain	8 Jun 1874	84	H Grove	South-east
Black, William W	"	Mate	8 Jun 1877	51	"	South
Blake, Charles F	"	Lt Comd'r	20 Feb 1879	35	Propr's	South—N W
Boardman, G Clifford	"	A A Paym'r	12 Nov 1865	25	"	North—C*
Bonnen, Peter	War 1812	Soldier	10 Dec 1867	85	Greenland	Bracket Fm
Bradford, Joseph M	U S Navy	Captain	14 Apr 1872	46	Propr's	North—C
Brewster, John W	4th N H	2 Lt Co B	27 Sep 1872	50	"	North—W
Briggs, Francis	U S Navy	....	....	...	H Grove	South-west
Brown, Charles H	1st N H H A	Serg Co A	10 Dec 1880	37	Riverside	Near gate*
Brown, George A	17 Ms & N H H A	Cp F & Sgt L	10 Feb 1880	39	H Grove	North-east
Brown, George W	13th N H	Priv Co K	5 Mar 1891	70	Newington	West
Brown, John W	"	Priv Co K	13 Aug 1887	...	Propr's	North—N E
Brown, Oren P	10th Mass Bat	Priv	9 Jul 1867	38	"	South—W
Buckley, Michael	U S Navy	Connecticut	4 Nov 1872	32	St Mary's	West
Carlton, Joseph W	"	Louisville	10 Sep 1865	21	H Grove	South-east
Carter, Henry M	16th N H	Priv Co K	24 Jun 1863	44	"	North-east
Case, Heman	1st Me H Art	Priv Co L	24 Aug 1886	40	Propr's	South—S
Caswell, Charles R	13th N H	Priv Co K	11 Nov 1865	34	Rye	Foss' Beach
Caswell, William	8 In 1 B Ms, 1 U S V	Pr (D S C I)	7 Jun 1867	...	"	"
Chace, Horace J	U S Navy	....	10 Aug 1864	20	H Grove	South-west
Chamberlain, Alb't Jr	"	....	2 Oct 1879	38	Propr's	North—S
Chase, Algernon F	2nd N H	Priv Co B	27 Aug 1862	21	Sagamore	South
Clark, Augustus L	U S Navy	....	6 Nov 1872	41	Greenland	Center
Clark, Charles H	U S N & N H H A	Priv Co K	31 Mar 1886	45	Chris Shore	Near Pond
Clark, George	Mass Vols	....	....	...	H Grove	North
Clark, George H	7th Mass & U S M C	Pr E & Corp	20 Dec 1883	42	Propr's	South—C
Clark, Thomas K	26th Mass	Priv Co C	....	...	North	West
Clough, Nathan	13th N H	Priv Co K	11 Jan 1872	59	Rye	Rye Center
Coffin, John N	8 Bat & 5 V M Ms	1 Lt & Cap B	6 Jul 1891	66	Propr's	South—S
Colby, John	3rd U S Art	Priv Co I	....	...	Tarlton's	East*
Cole, Edwin O	1st Me H Art	Priv Co L	7 Oct 1884	38	Sagamore	West
Cole, Levi W	4th N H & U S N	Priv Co H	6 Mar 1869	27	Riverside	Center
Collins, John	10th N H	Priv Co G	4 Aug 1884	64	St Mary's	North-east
Collins, Joseph	U S Navy	....	1 Jun 1868	40	"	South

Name.	Service.	Rank or Ship.	Died.	Age.	Cemetery.	Part.
Conners, John	U S Navy	....	23 Apr 1880	80	St Mary's	North
Connor, Benjamin	Rev War	Soldier	29 Dec 1835	87	Greenland	West
Cox, George	U S Navy	Mahaska	19 Mar 1892	67	H Grove	Center
Critchley, Thomas H	13th N H	Priv Co K	3 May 1886	40	Sagamore	South
Crowley, Michael	U S Navy	....	....	...	St Mary's	Center
Cunningham, Bernard	"	....	....	...	"	"
Currier, Willie H	3rd U S Art	Corp Co I	....	...	Propr's	North—S
Curtis, Charles H	13th N H	Capt Co F	19 Mar 1891	50	Riverside	West
Daily, Milo H	11th Mass Bat	Priv	19 Jun 1864	20	H Grove	South-east
Danielson, Fred	U S Navy	Colorado	....	...	"	East
Danielson, Joseph H	13th N H	Corp Co K	8 May 1877	45	"	"
David, George E	"	Priv Co K	30 Jan 1879	42	"	North
Davidson, James	"	Corp Co K	25 Dec 1884	57	"	"
Davidson, James	U S Art & N H V	Capt N H V	26 Sep 1874	74	Riverside	North-west
Davis, Alfred E	6th N H	Priv Co H	22 Jul 1892	50	Cotton s	" *
Davis, Lewis	10th N H	Priv Co G	20 Jun 1867	25	Tarlton's	Center
Davis, Thomas J	13th N H	Priv Co C	14 Jun 1864	25	"	"
Dearborn, George E	U S Navy	Colorado	6 Jun 1889	50	Greenland	South*
Dearborn, Samuel D	8th N H	Priv Co I	30 Jun 1884	74	"	"
Dennett, George F	19th Mass	Priv Co E	4 Sep 1864	33	Union	North-east
Dennett, Robert O	U S Navy	A 2 A Engr	9 Nov 1882	53	"	"
Dennett, Thomas S	U S Vols	Capt, Div Q	12 Sep 1863	38	"	"
Denny, John	U S Navy	....	....	...	Cotton's	North-west
DeWit Carsten B	"	Kearsarge	15 May 1865	56	Newington	East
Dimick, Justin	U S Army	Brig Gen	13 Oct 1871	71	Propr's	South—S W
Dimick, Justin E	2nd U S Art	1 Lt Bat H	5 May 1863	23	"	"
Dixon, John	U S Navy	....	27 Jan 1881	44	St Mary's	Center
Downing, Havillah F	Mex War & 6 N H	Cp 9 & Pr H	12 Jun 1874	50	North	West
Downing, John	U S Navy	....	....	...	"	South-east
Downing, Nelson N	"	Pensacola	24 Apr 1862	19	H Grove	"
Drew, Charles H	22nd Ms & U S N	Priv Co I	22 Dec 1880	40	Propr's	South—N*
Drew, Isaac C	16th N H	Priv Co K	....	...	H Grove	Center
Driver, Robert	18th Mass	Priv Co B	....	...	"	West
Dunn, Clarence	19th Mass	Priv Co D	21 Jun 1862	20	"	South-east
Edney, Charles A	16th N H	Music Co K	24 Aug 1863	18	"	South-west
Edney, George A	89th N Y	Priv Co H	8 Apr 1876	45	"	"
Emery, James H	16th N H	1 Serg Co K	5 Aug 1870	32	"	"
Engen, Peter	U S Navy	Vandalia	27 May 1890	53	St Mary's	North-west
Evans, Acanthus G	"	Ossipee	6 May 1886	38	Sagamore	West
Fall, Edwin H	32nd Mass	Priv Co I	2 Jul 1863	19	Propr's	North—N W
Falvey, John	2nd N H	Priv Co K	27 May 1873	48	St Mary's	South
Falvey, Timothy	U S M C	....	13 Feb 1883	62	"	South-west*
Fishley, George	Rev War	Soldier	26 Dec 1850	91	Propr's	North—C
Fitzgerald, Richard	10th N H	Priv Co G	27 Nov 1887	77	St Mary's	South-east
Flynn, John	N H Vols	Priv	25 May 1866	21	"	North-west
Ford, James E	15 N H & N H H A	Cp F & Sg L	29 Apr 1885	39	H Grove	East
Foss, Robert S	13th N H	Priv Co K	29 Oct 1891	66	Rye	Town Cem*
Foster, Robert F	23rd Mass	Priv Co C	19 Dec 1878	48	H Grove	South-west
Foye, John Harrison	13th N H	Priv Co E	3 May 1863	22	Rye	Sagamore
Foye, Thomas F	War 1812	Soldier	15 Mar 1881	84	Newington	East
Franklin, Fred A	3rd Md	Priv Co C	1 Oct 1887	80	Propr's	North—C
Franklin, Fred H	U S Navy	Colorado	10 May 1873	33	"	"
Freeland, John	17th N H	Priv Co B	16 Jan 1863	17	Greenland	East
Fretson, Richard	U S Navy	....	10 Apr 1865	52	H Grove	Center
Fuller, Theodore	War 1812	....	 1844	82	"	"
Gammon, James T	2nd N H	Corp Co K	28 Jan 1887	45	"	"
Gannon, Thomas	"	Priv Co K	30 Nov 1872	54	St Mary's	South
Gardner, Franklin E	10th N H	Priv Co G	3 Feb 1863	18	H Grove	North
Gardner, William	Rev War	Major	29 Apr 1831	83	Episcopal	West
Gates, Storer D	1st N H Cav	Serg Tr A	14 Jul 1882	48	Sagamore	South-west*
Gates, Warren G	3rd N H	Priv Co D	20 Nov 1863	36	North	South
Gay, Thomas S	U S Navy	Act Ensign	29 Mar 1886	49	H Grove	South-west
Gerrish, George A	1st N H Bat	Captain	1 Sept 1866	32	"	South
Gilpatrick, Reuben E	5th N H	Priv Co D	16 Nov 1886	48	Newington	North-east
Goodrich, Edwin R	2 N,H & U S Vols	C S,BB Gen	22 Apr 1892	66	H Grove	South-west*
Goodrich, J Nelson	U S Navy	Boatswain	12 Sep 1882	46	Propr's	North—C
Goodrich, Marco B	4th Cal	Priv Co D	7 Dec 1875	48	"	"
Goodwin, Ichabod	N H	War Gov	4 Jul 1882	87	"	"
Gookin, George E	24th Mass	Priv Co H	29 Sep 1868	38	H Grove	Center
Grant, Alexander	Mex War	Pr K 3 Art	4 Aug 1851	32	"	West
Grant, John	War 1812	... .	25 Oct 1856	73	Propr's	South—S
Grant, William W	Mex War	Columbus	20 May 1847	26	"	"
Gray, Henry D	1st N H H Art	Serg Co K	....	...	H Grove	Center
Green, Mark	Rev War	Soldier	18 Sep 1851	89	Union	North
Greenough, Robert F	29th Mass	Corp Co H	17 Sep 1862	23	North	"
Griffey, John	U S M C	Priv	21 Dec 1889	52	Propr's	South—C
Gunnison, Nathaniel	13th N H	Priv Co K	10 Jan 1861	30	"	North—S
Hadley, Allston W	U S Navy	Mass'ch'tts	21 Aug 1880	36	"	South—N
Hahir, James	10th & 2nd N H	Priv G & D	18 Sep 1868	21	St Mary's	Center
Ham, Henry E	30th Me & U S N	C Serg 30 Me	22 Jul 1867	22	H Grove	East
Ham, Mark G	U S Navy	Kearsarge	11 Mar 1869	51	"	South
Hamilton, John	5th & 27th Me	Pr F & Cor G	20 Apr 1864	46	Tarlton's	East*
Hammond, Pierpont	10th N H	Priv Co G	Sep 1861	...	North	West
Hanson, Frank B	14th Mass	Priv Co A	11 Jun 1863	29	H Grove	Center

Name.	Service.	Rank or Ship.	Died.	Age.	Cemetery.	Part.
Hanson, John K A	13th N H	Priv Co K	....	...	Propr's	South—C
Harding, Samuel, Jr	U S Navy	Act. Ensign	6 Mar 1879	36	"	North—S E
Harmon, John	13th N H	Priv Co K	8 Oct 1870	46	H Grove	East
Harmon, Luther	4th N H	Priv Co B	23 Dec 1863	20	"	North
Harris, John	U S M C	....	28 Oct 1887	57	St Mary's	South
Hartnett, John	U S Navy	Colorado	17 Nov 1875	33	"	South-west
Harvey, Thomas	Rev War	Soldier	18 Jan 1837	84	North	South-east
Haselton, Geo Ed	....	....	23 Jun 1862	19	H Grove	North-east
Haven, Nathaniel A	Rev War	Surgeon	13 Mar 1831	69	Propr's	North—N
Haven, N Parker	Phil City Cav	Priv 1st Tr	6 Nov 1869	33	"	"
Haven, S Cushman	162nd N Y	2 Lt Co B	25 Jun 1863	20	"	South—W*
Hazlett, William C	U S Navy	....	 1861	22	H Grove	South-west
Heheir, Thomas W	"	Mass'ch'tts	....	...	Propr's	South—S*
Henderson, George D	"	Chaplain	29 May 1875	42	"	North—S E
Hennessey, Daniel	"	....	25 Nov 1868	26	St Mary's	Center
Hewins, Otis W	10th N H	Priv Co G	....	...	H Grove	South
Hill, Alfred J	Mex War & 3 N H	Serg 9 & Adj	1 Apr 1889	84	"	South-west
Hill, John Edward	19th Mass	A Surgeon	11 Sep 1862	27	"	North east
Hodgdon, George E	10th N H & V R C	1 Lt G & Cap	11 Jun 1891	52	Sagamore	West*
Hodgdon, Harland P	10th N H & I C	Corp Co G	11 Oct 1865	29	North	South
Hodgdon, Henry C	13th N H	Priv Co K	23 Dec 1862	18	Gray Ridge	HodgdonFm
Hodgdon, William C	War 1812	Priv N H M	18 Feb 1886	94	Newington	Center
Holbrook, John A	U S Navy	Sailmaker	2 Jan 1866	38	Cotton's	West
Hook, William S	14th Maine	Priv Co ...	23 Jun 1876	56	H Grove	Center
Hough, Andrew J	U S Navy	Carpenter	2 Sep 1864	36	"	North
Howard, Ferd. M	Mass Vols	....	7 Sep 1865	...	St Mary's	North-west
Hoyt, Franklin C	Mex War	....	27 Feb 1882	72	H Grove	" *
Hunter, Hugh	U S Navy	Macedonian	27 Jul 1887	18	Cotton's	North-east
Huntress, Charles E	2nd N H	Priv Co K	20 Sep 1862	21	Gray Ridge	Dennett Fm
Huntress, Seth	4th N H	Priv Co B	....	...	North	West
Jackson, Hall	Rev War	Surg Army	28 Sep 1797	58	"	North
Jackson, John H	Mex War & 3 N H	Cap 9 & Col	10 Apr 1890	75	Propr's	South—N
Jarvis, John B	N Y Vols	....	3 Jan 1870	39	H Grove	Center
Jellison, Daniel M	13th N H	Priv Co K	19 Feb 1878	42	"	North-east
Jenkins, William D	U S Navy	Carpenter	14 Apr 1883	...	"	"
Jenness, Albion J	13th N H	Priv Co E	8 Aug 1863	16	"	East
Jervis, Edward	10th N H	Priv Co G	8 May 1888	70	Cotton's	North-west
Johnson, Abram A	U S Navy	Brooklyn	15 Jun 1892	56	Propr's	North—S*
Johnson, Charles E	3rd & 5th N H	Cp D & Pr C	5 Oct 1877	38	Cotton's	South-east
Jones, Michael	U S Navy	....	....	...	St Mary's	East
Kane, Dennis	6th N H	Priv Co H	19 Feb 1870	45	"	North-east
Kelenbeck, Christop'r	16th N H & U S N	Priv Co K	9 Sep 1888	59	H Grove	South-west*
Kennard, Nathaniel	Rev War	Army&Navy	24 Jun 1823	68	North	South
Kennedy, William	1st Mass H Art	Corp Co F	6 Oct 1880	43	H Grove	South-east
Kennison, William S	13th N H	Priv Co E	29 Apr 1883	66	Cotton's	North-west
Kent, John Horace	43rd Mass	Serg Co A	4 Mar 1888	59	Sagamore	"
Kimball, Charles H	17th & 2nd N H	Priv B & K	2 Sep 1883	55	H Grove	North-east
Laighton, Alfred S	2nd Mass Cav	Pr Cal 100	29 Jul 1863	19	Propr's	North—C
Laighton, Alfred S	U S Navy	Act Ensign	16 Jan 1865	27	H Grove	South-west
Laighton, Bennett	16th N H	Corp Co K	20 Aug 1863	20	Propr's	North—C
Laighton, William F	U S Navy	Carpenter	25 Jun 1879	63	"	"
Laighton, William M	"	"	23 May 1873	63	"	"
Lake, Dayton W	11th Maine	Priv Co I	26 Aug 1865	20	"	"
Langdon, John	Rev War	Colonel	18 Sep 1819	80	North	South
Lear, Nathaniel M	2nd N H	Priv Co K	7 Apr 1871	32	H Grove	East
Leary, Jeremiah O	U S M C	Priv	....	...	St Mary's	"
Leary, Timothy O	16 N H & U S M C	Priv Co K	22 Jun 1889	42	"	"
Leslie, George T	7th Ill Cav	Priv Tr B	...Jan 1864	23	H Grove	" *
Lester, David G	War 1812	....	...Feb 1877	77	"	"
Lewis, John C.	1st N H & U S N	Priv Co B	18 Mar 1833	50	Newington	North east*
Libby, George W	13th N H	Priv Co C	11 Jun 1883	45	Riverside	Center*
Locke, Edwin W	U S Navy	....	30 Apr 1869	26	H Grove	North-west
Locke, Fletcher D	"	Pay Clerk	12 Mar 1875	33	Propr's	North—S W
Locke, John H	5th N H	1 Serg Co B	15 Jun 1889	48	Sagamore	South-west
Locke, Joseph J	12th Maine	Priv Co K	25 May 1863	19	H Grove	"
Locke, William W	U S Navy	.....	5 Sep 1868	35	"	North-west
Lombard, Harry	40th Mass	Priv Co F	31 May 1888	52	Propr's	North—S
Long, Pierse	Rev War	Colonel	3 Apr 1789	50	"	North—E
Lynch, Timothy	U S Navy	.....	22 Feb 1887	55	St Mary's	South-west
Lyon, John H	"	Sonoma	8 Feb 1864	21	Chris Shore	Near Pond
Marden, John H	10th N H	Priv Co G	31 Dec 1877	54	North	South-east
Marden, John L	2nd Mass Cav	Priv Tr K	27 Aug 1864	38	H Grove	Center
Marshall, Chris J	2nd N H	Corp Co K	18 Aug 1870	31	"	West
Marston, Albert S	5th N H	Corp Co H	2 Jun 1891	50	"	South
Marston, Joshua B	35th Mass	Priv Co B	9 Jan 1891	67	Propr's	South—W
Mates, James	U S Navy	....	21 Feb 1874	35	St Mary's	East
Maxwell, Wm H H	5th N H	Corp Co K	6 Apr 1865	24	H Grove	South-west
McClintock, Henry M	War 1812	Midshipm'n	24 Jul 1817	19	Propr's	North—E
McClintock, John	Rev War	Pr ArmShip	13 Nov 1855	94	"	"
McClintock, Samuel	"	Chaplain	27 Apr 1804	72	Greenland	North
McClure, James G	U S M C	....	23 Jan 1882	41	St Mary's	"
McDonald, James	U S N & U S M C	Kearsarge	21 Sep 1890	45	"	North-west*
McDuffee, John	U S Navy	....	....	...	Cotton's	South-west
McKone, James	"	....	21 Jan 1870	32	St Mary's	West

S

Name.	Service.	Rank or Ship.	Died.	Age.	Cemetery.	Part.
McLeond, John	U S Navy	De Soto	26 Aug 1868	36	Cotton's	North-west
McPherson, Alex'der	U S M C	Corp	18 Jun 1887	74	St Mary's	East
Mead, Cornelius	U S Navy	....	....	...	"	Center
Mead, Patrick	16 Mass & V R C	Priv Co D	....	...	"	South-east
Melmoth, Hector	U S M C	....	......	...	Riverside	East*
Merrill, George A	U S Navy	....	18 Oct 1867	25	Ch's Shore	Near Pond
Mills, William J	16th N H	Priv Co K	15 Apr 1889	75	H Grove	Center*
Mitchell, James	"	Priv Co K	9 Aug 1863	...	"	West
Moore, Andrew J	35th Mass	Priv Co K	17 Sep 1862	26	"	North
Moore, John	13th N H	Corp Co K	23 May 1879	39	"	South-west
Moore, John H	10th N H	Priv Co G	2 Jul 1864	24	"	North
Moore, Thomas R	U S Navy	Cumberl'd	11 Feb 1883	37	Sagamore	North-west
Moore, William	Mass Vols	Priv	20 Oct 1883	75	"	East
Morrill, John D	16th N H	1 Serg Co K	17 Jul 1873	38	Propr's	North—S W
Morrison, John H	10th N H	Priv Co G	3 Nov 1862	23	St Mary's	Center
Morse, Edgar L	4th Mass	Priv Co K	23 Jul 1878	33	H Grove	South-west
Moses, Edward	U S Navy	Act Master	18 May 1864	50	Propr's	North—E
Moses, Levi Jr	"	Flag	24 Sep 1861	35	"	"
Moulton, Charles W	3rd N H	Serg Co K	14 Mar 1872	33	North	North-west
Moulton, David A	U S N & 2 Ms C	Priv Tr A	....	...	Sagamore	North
Moulton, Thomas	Mex War	Portsmouth	18 Oct 1889	77	H Grove	South-west*
Murray, John	Mex War & 5 N H	3 Art & Capt	13 Dec 1862	37	Tarlton's	Center
Nash, Joseph E	16th N H	Priv Co K	30 May 1884	52	Cotton's	North-west
Neal, Franklin W	"	Priv Co K	21 Feb 1885	59	Riverside	East*
Nellings, William	U S M C	Corp	29 May 1873	...	H Grove	South-west
Newkirk, Peter	20th Mass	Serg Co A	27 Oct 1864	34	"	North
Norton, James	19th Mass	Priv Co E	3 Jan 1877	40	St Mary's	Center
Norton, James	"	Priv Co H	23 Apr 1887	...	"	East
Nowell, Andrew C	8th N H	Priv Co D	16 Aug 1862	32	H Grove	South
Noyes, Leverett W	U S Navy	Sonoma	31 Mar 1872	31	Newington	Center
Nutter, William H	13th N H	Priv Co E	....	...	Propr's	North—S
Olney, Jesse	3rd U S Art	Priv Co I	....	...	Tarlton's	East
Oxford, William F	2nd N H	Priv Co K	5 Aug 1861	23	H Grove	"
Palmer, Nathaniel F	"	Priv Co K	9 Aug 1862	19	"	South
Parker, William A	U S Navy	Captain	24 Oct 1882	66	"	Center
Parks, Edward H	"	Vandalia	11 Nov 1889	49	Propr's	South—N
Parks, J S	"	....	....	...	"	"
Parks, Thomas B	13th N H	Priv Co K	16 Mar 1863	18	North	West
Parrott, Enoch G	U S Navy	R Admiral	10 May 1879	63	Episcopal	"
Partridge, George F	"	....	23 Mar 1879	49	Sagamore	"
Patch, Charles W	2nd N H	2 Lt Co K	10 Jul 1863	33	H Grove	South-east
Paul, Joseph W	1st N H H Art	Corp Co A	15 Jun 1880	...	"	North
Payne, Albert L	16th N H	Priv Co K	8 Jul 1886	44	"	South-west
Pearson, George F	U S Navy	R Admiral	1 Jul 1867	71	"	East
Pearson, John H	16th N H	Priv Co K	22 Aug 1863	19	"	"
Pender, William P	10th N H	Priv Co A	16 May 1864	18	Propr's	South—N
Pendexter, Edward	U S Navy	Act Ensign	18 Nov 1870	27	"	North—N
Perkins, George	War 1812	Portsmouth	 1815	26	"	North—C
Perry, George N	U S Navy	....	....	...	North	South-east
Peterson, Adrian A	"	Gunner	27 Jul 1871	85	Propr's	North—W
Pettigrew, William	Mex War	U S Navy	9 Feb 1865	59	North	West
Pettigrew, William	U S Navy	....	5 Feb 1888	59	H Grove	South
Philbrick, Oliver B	13th N H	Priv Co K	21 Apr 1884	71	Rye	Rye Beach
Pickering, Charles W	U S Navy	Commodore	29 Feb 1888	72	H Grove	South
Pickering, Simeon S	"	Vanderbilt	12 Aug 1889	58	Propr's	South—N W*
Place, Charles S	"	....	20 Jan 1887	64	H Grove	South
Place, Leonard	"	Constellat'n	12 Jan 1877	62	"	"
Plaisted, B Frank P	"	....	20 Jan 1876	28	"	North-east
Plaisted, Charles E	2nd N H	Capt Co B	25 Apr 1874	35	"	South-west
Plaisted, William A	36th Mass	Priv Co C	26 Feb 1887	59	"	Center
Poole, John	20th Maine	Corp Co E	22 May 1881	59	Rye	Foss' Beach
Pottle, Samuel A	U S Navy	....	20 May 1885	38	Cotton's	North-west
Quint, Wm Goodwin	2nd N H	Priv Co K	19 Jun 1864	28	Newington	East
Ramsdell, John H	3rd U S Art	.... Co I	31 Mar 1868	20	H Grove	South
Ramsdell, S	"	Priv Co I	 1866	...	Tarlton's	East*
Rand, Ammi C	17th & 2nd N H	Priv B & A	....	...	H Grove	North
Rand, Francis W	9th N H	Priv Co E	20 Jan 1864	24	"	South-west
Rand, Irving	6th N H	Serg Co H	2 Aug 1864	25	Rye	Laf'y'tte R'd
Rand, Robert	13th N H	Priv Co K	13 Jan 1865	34	H Grove	North-west
Randall, Charles W	U S N & 13th N H	Priv Co K	22 Aug 1887	50	"	South
Randall, Reuben S	War 1812	....	10 Sep 1862	68	"	"
Rice, William A	83rd N Y	Serg Co D	9 Oct 1866	25	Propr's	North—N W*
Richards, Henry L	2nd U S Sharps	Serg Co F	4 Jul 1863	39	"	South—W
Ridge, Charles	2nd N H	Priv Co K	9 Jan 1879	61	H Grove	East
Ridge, Thomas W	U S Navy	Constellat'n	20 Oct 1879	32	"	"
Rogers, Joseph W	2nd N H	Priv Co K	13 Jan 1865	34	"	Center
Rokes, Lincoln	10th N H	Priv Co G	9 Feb 1875	57	Greenland	South
Ross, Charles H	U S Navy	Pensacola	17 Jul 1876	...	Propr's	North—S
Russell, John	"	....	26 Jan 1890	60	H Grove	South*
Rutter, Thomas	10th N H	Priv Co G	21 May 1883	67	"	North-east
Salisbury, Wm Henry	....	Priv	7 Nov 1868	26	"	South-west
Salmon, Thomas	U S Navy	Kearsarge	8 Oct 1882	59	Calvary	North-west*
Sawyer, George	1st Mass	Corp Co G	6 Dec 1875	38	H Grove	South-east
Sawyer, Samuel	23rd Mass	Priv Co K	24 May 1885	48	"	Center

Name.	*Service.*	*Rank or Ship.*	*Died.*	*Age.*	*Cemetery.*	*Part.*
Saxton, Mortimer F	30th Mass	Priv Co H	11 Oct 1862	39	H Grove	East
Seaver, John W	47th Mass	Priv Co F	5 Dec 1873	33	"	South-west
Seavey, Joseph J	19th Mass	Priv Co F	29 Mar 1888	50	Sagamore	South
Seymour, Frank	4th N Y Art	1 Lt Co L	23 Jul 1876	45	Propr's	South—S
Shapley, John H	1st N H Cav	1 Serg Tr M	28 Sep 1864	25	Rye	Breakf't Hill
Shapley, Robert P	"	1 Lt Tr M	2 Jun 1865	29	"	"
Shaw, John	16th N H	Priv Co K	....	...	Cotton's	South-west
Sherburne, John C	10th N H	Priv Co G	10 Dec 1877	72	H Grove	Center
Shillaber, Robert E	1st N H Cav	Q Sgt Tr M	7 Jul 1865	23	Propr's	North—S
Shock, Thomas A	U S Navy	Chief Engr	11 Jan 1873	41	H Grove	West
Shuttleworth, Wm	U S M C	....	8 Sep 1887	54	"	Center
Sides, George L	13th N H	Priv Co K	5 Aug 1889	47	"	North-east
Small, Robert	U S M C	Sergeant	26 Sep 1867	58	"	South
Smart, George E	U S Navy	Kearsarge	....	...	"	North
Smith, James	3rd U S Art	Priv Co K	1 Oct 1878	52	Tarlton's	East*
Smith, William	Mex War	....	18 Dec 1856	58	H Grove	North
Snow, James B	U S Navy	Ossipee	11 Sep 1865	53	Propr's	North—S W
Spalding, Champion	War 1812	Lt N H M	28 Oct 1814	26	North	North-west
Spalding, Lyman G	U S Navy	Lieutenant	29 Aug 1881	36	Propr's	South—N W
Spinney, George A	6 Inf & 1 Cav Ms	Priv K & D	17 Jun 1863	25	"	South—W
Spinney, Horace S	13th N H	Priv Co K	....	42	H Grove	North
Stack, Michael F	U S Navy	De Soto	11 Jul 1877	37	St Mary's	East
Staples, Samuel	57th Mass	Priv Co D	....	...	H Grove	South-west
Stearns, James	5th N H	Corp Co K	12 Dec 1887	48	"	North
Storer, George W	U S Navy	R Admiral	8 Jan 1864	74	Propr's	North—N W
Storer, Robert B	Mex War	Midshipm'n	4 Jul 1847	22	"	"
Stott, George	13th N H	Priv Co K	24 Jun 1892	75	Sagamore	East
Stott, Robert A	17th & 2nd N H	Priv B & K	4 Jul 1890	44	"	"
Stringer, Joseph W	U S Navy	....	27 Sep 1862	21	North	West
Sullivan, Peter	10th N H	Priv Co G	8 Aug 1891	57	Calvary	North-west*
Sweeney, Barney	N H H Art	Priv 1st Co	21 Oct 1863	...	Tarlton's	East*
Talham, Charles A	2nd N H	Priv Co D	27 Sep 1862	27	H Grove	South-east
Taylor, Alfred	U S Navy	R Admiral	19 Apr 1891	81	Propr's	South—S W*
Taylor, George	13th N H	Corp Co K	26 May 1874	39	Sagamore	West
Tetherly, Andrew	U S Navy	....	29 Mar 1864	24	H Grove	South-west
Thacher, Joseph H	16th N H	Capt Co K	5 Jan 1892	67	"	South*
Thompson, —	3rd U S Art	Priv Co K	....	...	Tarlton's	East*
Thompson, Thomas	Rev War	Capt U S N	22 Feb 1809	68	North	Center*
Towle, George W	10th N H	Capt Co G	20 Apr 1887	76	H Grove	South east
Tredick, John H	3rd N H	2 Lt Co E	6 Jul 1864	32	"	North
Tucker, Charles H	27th Maine	Corp Co B	3 Jul 1879	39	Sagamore	"
Tucker, Henry	U S Navy	....	....	...	Propr's	North—S
Tucker, John A	3rd N H	Corp Co D	1 Dec 1886	48	Greenland	South
Tucker, Mark W	16th N H	Priv Co K	8 Feb 1863	26	H Grove	"
Tufts, John P	40th N Y	Priv Co H	17 Aug 1879	...	"	North
Upham, Joseph B Jr	U S Navy	P A Engr	14 Aug 1889	48	Propr's	North—C
Upham, Timothy	War 1812	Lt Col 21 U S	2 Nov 1855	72	"	"
Varney, Charles L	U S Navy	....	4 Aug 1870	28	H Grove	North east
Waldren, Samuel W	16th N H	Priv E & K	24 Aug 1863	33	"	South-west
Waldron, N S	Mex War	Br Maj M C	21 Feb 1857	52	Propr's	South—W
Waldron, Samuel W jr	31st N Y & U S Vols	Capt & A A G	24 Aug 1882	53	"	North—S
Walker, Wm Augustus	27th Mass	Major	3 Jun 1864	36	"	North—C
Wallace, Joseph	U S Navy	....	....	...	Sagamore	West
Walsh, James	"	Shawsheen	2 Sep 1865	...	H Grove	East
Walsh, Richard	10th N H & U S N	Priv Co G	17 Jul 1864	30	St Mary's	West
Warburton, William	13th N H	Priv Co K	9 Jul 1882	61	Propr's	South—S
Watkins, Benjamin F	16th N H	Priv Co K	4 Feb 1863	22	"	North—S
Watkins, Daniel W	"	Priv Co K	13 Sep 1863	22	H Grove	East
Webster, Henry C	U S Navy	Mate	23 Sep 1862	22	Sagamore	North
Webster, Mark R	War 1812	Soldier	13 Jul 1865	74	"	South-west
Whaley, Wm Henry	10th & 2nd N H	Sg I & Pr D	21 Jun 1880	41	Greenland	South*
Whidden, Andrew W	10th N H	Priv Co G	27 Jan 1865	20	H Grove	North-west
Whipple, Amiel W	U S Army	Maj Gen	7 May 1863	45	Propr's	North—W
Whipple, Prince	Rev War	Gen Staff	 1797	...	North	South*
Whipple, William	"	Signer	28 Nov 1785	55	"	Center
White, John	7th N H	Priv Co G	12 Apr 1892	65	Cotton's	North-west*
Whitehouse, Eben E	War 1812	....	24 Jul 1862	62	H Grove	West
Whitehouse, Sam'l N	U S Navy	Carpenter	2 Jan 1891	56	"	"
Whittier, Samuel C	11 & 23 Mass	Surgeon	1 Feb 1893	56	Propr's	South—W*
Wholley, James	30th Mass	Priv Co E	8 Nov 1888	47	St Mary's	East
Wiggin, Samuel P	War 1812	....	16 May 1853	56	North	South
Willey, Henry J	10th N H	Serg Co G	12 Sep 1873	38	H Grove	Center
Willey, John	War 1812	....	16 Mar 1880	82	"	North-east
Wilson, Robert	U S Navy	....	5 May 1884	37	Sagamore	North-west
Wingate, William	10th N H	Priv Co G	....	...	H Grove	South-west
Wood, Charles A	U S M C	Fifer	....	...	"	North
Yates, Arthur R	U S Navy	Captain	4 Nov 1891	53	Propr's	South—E
Yeaton, John B	1st U S Art	Serg Co B	16 Jan 1874	36	Riverside	East
Young, Charles E	1st N H H Art	Priv Co A	24 Jul 1888	58	H Grove	East*
Young, George B	44th Mass	Priv Co G	2 Feb 1863	23	"	North-east
Young, Willard W	26th Maine	Priv Co C	19 May 1883	53	"	South
Young, William C	Mex War	Raritan	6 Jan 1869	50	North	West*

PORTSMOUTH.

Cemetery			
Calvary Cemetery		2	
Cotton's "		14	
Episcopal "		2	
Harmony Grove "		156	
North "		25	
Proprietors' "		85	
Sagamore "		21	
St. Mary's "		39	
Union "		4	
Christian Shore, Private Ground		3	
Gravelly Ridge, "		2	
			353

NEIGHBORING TOWNS.

Town			
Greenland { Brackett Farm	1	10	
Greenland { Town Cemetery	9		
Newcastle, Riverside Cemetery		8	
" Tarlton's "		10	
Newington—Town Cemetery		11	
Rye { Breakfast Hill	2	10	
Rye { Foss' Beach	3		
Rye { Lafayette Road	1		
Rye { Rye Beach	1		
Rye { Rye Center	1		
Rye { Sagamore	1		
Rye { Town Cemetery	1		
			49
Total			402

NOTE.

Allen, William	See Pender, William P.
Barnes, James	See Franklin, Fred H.
Berry, William H.	See Barry, William H.
Brown, George T.	See Leslie, George T.
Goodwin, William H.	See Quint, William Goodwin
Harvey, John	See Falvey, John
Jarvis, Edward	See Jervis, Edward
Lombard, Henry	See Lombard, Harry
Noyes, Joseph	See Noyes, Leverett W.
O'Leary, Timothy	See Leary, Timothy O.
Parks, David	See Parks, Edward H.
Simpson, John	See Whaley, William Henry
Welch Richard	See Walsh, Richard

IN HONOR OF THE MEN

OF

PORTSMOUTH

WHO GAVE

THEIR SERVICES ON THE
LAND AND ON THE SEA
IN THE WAR WHICH
PRESERVED THE UNION
OF THE STATES THIS
MONUMENT IS ERECTED
BY GRATEFUL CITIZENS.

1888.

ANTIETAM GETTYSBURG

FREDERICKSBURG KEARSARGE

WILLIAMSBURG
FAIR OAKS
SAVAGE STATION
WHITE OAK SWAMP
MALVERN HILL
CHANTILLY
SOUTH MOUNTAIN
CHANCELLORSVILLE
WILDERNESS
COLD HARBOR
PETERSBURG
RICHMOND
MONITOR & MERRIMACK
NEW ORLEANS
MOBILE BAY
MORRIS ISLAND
JAMES ISLAND
FORT DARLING
PORT HUDSON
RED RIVER
FORT DONELSON
PEACH TREE CREEK
SHERMAN'S MARCH TO THE SEA

Soldiers' and Sailors' Monument, Portsmouth, N. H.

LINCOLN'S SPEECH AT GETTYSBURG.

NOVEMBER 19, 1863.

"Fourscore and seven years ago our fathers brought forth on this continent, a new nation, conceived in liberty, and dedicated to the proposition that all men are created equal. Now we are engaged in a great civil war, testing whether that nation, or any nation so conceived and so dedicated, can long endure. We are met on a great battle-field of that war. We have come to dedicate a portion of that field, as a final resting-place for those who here gave their lives that that nation might live. It is altogether fitting and proper that we should do this. But, in a larger sense, we cannot dedicate—we cannot consecrate—we cannot hallow—this ground. The brave men, living and dead, who struggled here, have consecrated it, far above our poor power to add or detract. The world will little note, nor long remember, what we say here, but it can never forget what they did here. It is for us the living, rather, to be dedicated here to the unfinished work which they who fought here have thus far so nobly advanced. It is rather for us to be here dedicated to the great task remaining before us—that from these honored dead we take increased devotion to that cause for which they gave the last full measure of devotion—that we here highly resolve that these dead shall not have died in vain—that this nation, under God, shall have a new birth of freedom—and that government of the people, by the people, for the people, shall not perish from the earth."

Appleton's Cyclopedia of American Biography.

THE GRAVES WE DECORATE.

ADDITIONAL RECORDS.

The Regiments are Infantry unless otherwise stated.

Abbott, George Clark—U. S. Navy.

Son of "John E. and Susan Abbott. . . . Killed in Texas." *Stone.*

"Boatswain, 31 January, 1862. Resigned 3 April, 1866."

Hamersly's General Navy Register.

Abbott, Samuel P.—13th N. H.

"Private Co. K. Residence or assignment, Portsmouth. Date of Muster Sept. 20, 1862, for 3 years. Discharged for disability at Washington, D. C., February 23, 1863."

Adjutant General's Records, N. H.

Adams, Charles F.—13th N. H.

"Son of Josiah and Frances D. Adams" *Stone.*

"Private Co. E. Residence or assignment, Portsmouth. Date of Muster, Sept. 23, 1862, for 3 years. Promoted to Sergeant, Sept. 6, 1864. Wounded slightly at Chapin's Farm, Va., Sept. 30, 1864. Mustered out, June 21, 1865."

Adjutant General's Records, N. H.

Adams, Horace H.—10th N. H.

"Wounded at Fair Oaks, Oct. 27, died at Hampton Hospital, Va., Nov. 10, 1864. . . . Son of Josiah and Frances D. Adams."

"Another soldier gone,
Another heart-beat stilled,
And once again, fond loving hearts
With anguish have been filled.

But while we mourn let us look up
And smiling through our pain,
Remember, what to us is loss,
To him is heavenly gain."

Stone.

"Private Co. G. Residence or assignment, Portsmouth. Date of Muster, Sept. 4, 1862, for 3 years. Promoted to Corporal, Oct. 30, 1863. Wounded severely, Oct. 27, 1864. Died of wounds, Nov. 9, 1864 [See above]."

Adjutant General's Records, N. H.

Adams, John Frank—27th Maine.

Enlisted as "John F. Adams."

"Eldest son of Samuel and Mary J. Adams. Died in Boston, Mass."

Stone.

"Private Co. G. Born in Portsmouth, N. H. Resident of Kittery, Maine. Date of Muster, Sept. 30, 1862, for 9 months. Mustered out and honorably discharged July 17, 1863, at Portland, Maine, by reason of expiration of term of service."

Adjutant General's Records, Maine.

Adams, Patrick—6th N. H.

"Private Co. H. Recruit. Residence or assignment, Henniker. [Actual residence, Portsmouth]. Date of Muster, June 8, 1864, for 3 years. Wounded at Petersburg, Va., July 5, 1864. Discharged on account of wounds, June 12, 1865."

Adjutant General's Records, N. H.

"Patrick, better known as 'Yankee,' Adams, died [in Portsmouth] on Saturday [Oct. 15, 1892]. . . . Adams served in the war of the rebellion. . . . Four years ago he broke one of his legs, which necessitated his going to the Soldier's Home at Togus, Me., where he remained until within a few weeks, when he came to this city."

Portsmouth Daily News, Oct. 17, 1892.

Adams, William C.—War 1812.

He was captured at sea, and was a prisoner of war at Dartmoor, England.

Amazeen, Joseph—U. S. R. M.

"Commissioned 3rd Lieutenant U. S. Revenue Marine, April 13, 1837. 2nd

Lieutenant, December 9, 1839. 1st Lieutenant, September 1, 1846. On account of a reduction in the number of officers his commission was vacated June 11, 1849.

Recommissioned 3rd Lieutenant, July 8, 1854. 2nd Lieutenant. March 10, 1855. 1st Lieutenant. April 5, 1855. Reduced to 2nd Lieutenant, January 9, 1862. Commissioned 1st Lieutenant, July 1, 1863. Captain July 11, 1864. Died April 20, 1880.

During the period of the war of the Rebellion he served on vessels and stations as follows. viz:

May to September, 1861, 'Cushing,' Portland, Maine; September 1861 to April 1862, waiting orders: April 1862 to June 1863, 'Black,' Boston, Mass.: June 1863 to June 1864, 'Agassiz' and 'Forward,' inland waters of North Carolina; June 1864 to September 1864, 'Pawtuxet,' New York; September 1864 to close of war, 'Agassiz,' New Bedford Mass."

Records Treasury Department.

Anderson, James F.—16th N. H.

Enlisted as "James Anderson."

"Private Co. K. Residence Portsmouth. Date of Muster, Nov. 8, 1862, for 9 months. Mustered out. August 20, 1863."

Adjutant General's Records, N. H.

Anderson, James F.— . . .

"Son of John and Sarah A. Anderson. . . . Faithful and true."

Stone.

Anderson, John—Mex. War.

"Died at Mexico, . . . A kind husband and affectionate father." *Stone.*

Atchison, George C.—U. S. Navy.

"George C. Aitchision." *Stone.*

Austin, Benj. M.— . .

Ayers, James S.—10th N. H.

"Private Co. G. Residence or assignment. Portsmouth. Date of Muster Sept. 1, 1862, for 3 years. Promoted to Corporal, Dec. 1, 1862. Discharged for disability, March 30, 1863."

Adjutant General's Records, N. H.

Bailey, Geo. F.—6 Inf. & 1 Cav. Mass.

"A member of the 6th Mass. Regt. three months, reënlisted in 1st Mass. Cavalry to the end of the war." *Stone.*

"Private Co. F. 6th Mass. Infantry. Residence, Lawrence, Mass. Enlisted ——. Date of Muster, April 22, 1861, for 3 months. Discharged Aug. 2, 1861, expiration of service.

Private Troop D, 1st Mass. Cavalry. Residence, Lawrence, Mass. Enlisted Sept. 16, 1861. Date of Muster Sept. 17, 1861, for 3 years. Reënlisted Jan. 1, 1864. Promoted to Corporal. March 19, 1864. On detached service, at Richmond, Va. Mustered out June, 29, 1865, with Company."

Adjutant General's Records, Mass.

Bailey, William—U. S. Navy.

"The beloved son of James and Elizabeth Bailey, born at Barnard Castle, England." *Stone.*

Banks, John S.—

Banks, Orrin—War 1812.

Barnes, William A.—U. S. Navy.

Enlisted as "William Barnes."

Member Storer Post, G. A. R.

Landsman U. S. Steamer "Kearsarge."

"Seaman. Birthplace Newfoundland. Enlisted Oct. 5, 1862. U. S. Steamer 'Kearsarge.' Discharged Nov. 29, 1864, ship went out of commission."

Post Records.

One of the crew of the U. S. Steamer "Kearsarge" when she destroyed the "Alabama," off Cherbourg. France, June 19, 1864. See record of Mark G. Ham.

Barr, Ferdinand—13th N. H.

"Private Co. K. Residence or assignment. Portsmouth. Date of Muster Sept. 20, 1862, for 3 years. Mustered out May 28, 1865."

Adjutant General's Records, N. H.

Barry, William H.—1st N. H. H. Art.

Enlisted as "William H. Berry."

"Private Co. A. Residence or assignment. Portsmouth. Date of Muster July 2, 1863. for 3 years. Mustered out Sept. 11, 1865."

Adjutant General's Records, N. H.

Barsantee, Alphonzo—2d Mass. Bat.

Enlisted as "Alphonso Barsantee."

"Son of John and Ezoa Barsantee."

Stone.

"Private. Residence, Boston. Enlisted July 31, 1861. Date of Muster. July 31, 1861. for 3 years. Mustered out Aug. 16, 1864."

Adjutant General's Records, Mass.

Barsantee, John B.—War 1812.

"Died in Boston, Mass."
Portsmouth Chronicle, Sept. 4, 1875.

The Letter of Marque on which he served was captured by the British, and he was a prisoner of war at Dartmoor, England. *Family Traditions.*

Bartow, Theodore B.—U. S. Navy.

"Theodore Beekman Bartow . . . died May 17, 1869." *Stone.*

"Chaplain, 6 September, 1841. Died 18 May [see above] 1869."
Hamersly's General Navy Register.

"Died at Portsmouth, N. H., May 18, [see above] 1869."
Navy Register, 1870.

Bates, Patrick—U. S. M. C.

His stone reads incorrectly—"Pat'k Bates, U. S. Navy."

Bates, Robert—U. S. M. C.

"Sergeant Robert Bates, U. S. M. C. retired, [who died in Kittery, Maine, July 11, 1892] . . . was 60 years of age and a native of Vermont. He formerly resided in this city, moving to Kittery about 8 years ago.

He has an honorable record as a veteran soldier, and will be buried tomorrow by E. G. Parker Post, G. A. R. [of Kittery, of which he was a member]. A sergeant's guard of marines from the Navy Yard will also attend the funeral."
Portsmouth Daily Evening Post, July 12, 1892.

Baxter, George D.—1st N. Y. Art.

Enlisted as "George Baxter."

Member Storer Post, G. A. R.

"Private, Co. G. Enlisted Sept. 29, 1861, for 3 years. Dropped from the rolls per G. O. No. 3, Artillery Headquarters. Army of Potomac, October 7, 1863."
Adjutant General's Records, N. Y.

"Born in Scotland, 1812." Discharged on account of "a gun shot wound in the right shoulder."
Soldiers Memorial 1889.

Beal, Freeman G.—U. S. Navy.

Bennett, Abner B.—U. S. Army.

"Surgeon, Hospital, Point of Rocks, Va." *Records Storer Post.*

Benson, Charles A.—U. S. Navy.

Berry, Albert C.—4th N. H.

"Private Co. B. Residence Portsmouth. Date of Muster, Sept. 18, 1861, for 3 years. Reenlisted Feb. 20, 1864. Sergeant Co. B. Date of Muster, Feb. 20, 1864, for 3 years. Captured at Drury's Bluff, Va., May 29, 1864 Paroled Nov. 24, 1864. Promoted to First Sergeant, March 1, 1865. Mustered out July 28, 1865."
Adjutant General's Record, N. H.

Bickford, Andrew—Mex. War.

"Private Co. C., 9th U. S. Infantry. Residence, Dover. Enlisted April 2, 1847, to serve during the war."
Adjutant General's Report, N. H. 1868.

Binch, David—9th N. H.

"Private Co. C. Residence Portsmouth. Date of Muster, July 17, 1862, for 3 years. Died of disease at Nicholasville, Kentucky, Sept 6, 1863"
Adjutant General's Records, N. H.

Bishop, Henry J.—U. S. M. C.

"Second Lieutenant, 25 November, 1861. First Lieutenant, 1 April, 1864. Captain, 12 January, 1876."
Hamersly's General Navy Register.

"Died at Brooklyn, N. Y., December 22, 1884." *Navy Register, 1885.*

"Born in Connecticut. Commisioned as Second Lieutenant, November 25, 1861; Marine Barracks, Brooklyn, 1862-3; 'Vermont,' South Atlantic Blockading Squadron, 1863-4. Commissioned as First Lieutenant. April 1, 1864: Marine Baracks, Portsmouth, 1865-6; steam sloop 'Susquehanna,' special cruise, 1866-7; Marine Barracks, Portsmouth, 1867-8; Marine Barracks, Pensacola, 1868-9; steamsloop 'California', Pacific Fleet, 1870-1, and 'Pensacola' same station, 1871-2; receiving ship 'Vermont,' 1874-5; receiving ship 'Colorado,' 1875-6. Commissioned as Captain, 1876; flagship 'Hartford,' North Atlantic Station, 1877-9; receiving ship 'Colorado,' 1879-80."
Hamersly's Naval Encyclopedia.

Black, William—U. S. Navy.

"Boatswain, 30 March, 1835. Died 8 June, 1874,"
Hamersly's General Navy Register.

"Died at Melrose, Mass., June 8, 1874."
Navy Register, 1875.

Black, William W.—U. S. Navy.

"Mate, 23 September. 1862. Resigned, 14 June, 1864."
Hamersly's General Navy Register.

Blake, Charles F.—U. S. Navy.

Charles Follen Blake.

"Acting Midshipman, 26 October, 1859. Ensign, 26 June, 1863. Master [Lieutenant—see below], 22 February, 1864 Lieutenant-Commander, 25 July, 1866. Retired list, 18 January, 1871. Died 20 February, 1879."

Hamersly's General Navy Register.

"Died at North Platte, Nebraska, February 20, 1879." *Navy Register 1880.*

"Born in Massachusetts. Appointed from Massachusetts, October 26, 1859; Naval Academy, 1859-61: Attached to steam-sloop 'Mississippi,' Atlantic coast, 1861; sloop 'Constellation,' Mediterranean squadron, 1862-3.

Promoted to Ensign, June 26 1863; West Gulf Blockading Squadron, 1864; battle of Mobile Bay, August 5, 1864.

Commissioned as Lieutenant, February 22, 1864; steam-sloop 'Powhatan,' Pacific Squadron, 1865-8.

Commissioned as Lieutenant-Commander, July 25, 1866; Naval Academy, 1868-70." *Hamersly's Naval Records, 1878.*

Boardman, G. Clifford—U. S. Navy.

George Clifford Boardman, son of Dr. John H. and Susan (Rice) Boardman, and grandson of Hon. Langley Boardman.

"Langley Boardman—1831." *Tomb.*

"Acting Assistant Paymaster, 23 July, 1862. Died 12 November, 1865."

Hamersly's General Navy Register.

"Died on U. S. Steamer 'Rhode Island,' November, 12, 1865."

Navy Register, 1866.

"On Wednesday morning [November 22, 1865] ex-Governor Goodwin received a dispatch from Secretary Welles, stating that Paymaster Boardman died at Havana on the 12th inst.—George Clifford Boardman, Paymaster, U. S. N., was a son of Dr. Boardman of this city: he was about twenty-five years of age, and a young man of more than ordinary promise. He was attached to the ex-rebel steamer 'Stonewall,' which vessel has put into Beaufort. His disease was yellow fever."

Portsmouth Journal Nov. 25, 1865.

He served as an Acting Assistant Paymaster, U. S. Navy, on board the steamer "Norwich" in the South Atlantic Blockading Squadron for about two years, and on the steamer "Galena." In the autumn of 1865 he was ordered to the ex-rebel ironclad "Stonewall" at Havana, when that vessel, surrendered to the Spaniards by her commander at the end of the war, was by them turned over to the United States. He went to Havana in the U. S. Steamer "Rhode Island," Commander Alexander Murray, (afterwards Rear Admiral,) and died at Havana, of yellow fever, November 12, 1865.

Bonnen, Peter—War 1812.

Enlisted as "Peter Bonner."

"A soldier in the war of 1812. . . . A faithful friend." *Stone.*

"Private, Capt. Robert Neal's company of Artillery of N. H. Militia. Enlisted June 28, 1812. Discharged August 31, 1812."

Adjutant General's Report, N. H., 1868-Part 2.

Buried on farm of S. S. Brackett, Bayside, Greenland, N. H.

Bradford, Joseph M.—U. S. Navy.

"Midshipman, 10 January, 1840. Passed Midshipman, 11 July, 1846. Master, 1 March 1855. Lieutenant, 14 September, 1855. Lieutenant-Commander, 16 July 1862. Commander, 25 July 1866. Retired list 5 February, 1872. Captain, Retired list, 16 March 1872. Died, 14 April 1872."

Hamersly's General Navy Register.

"Died at Norfolk, Virginia, April 14 1872."

Navy Register, 1873.

"Born in Tennessee. Appointed from Alabama, January 10, 1840: attached to frigate 'Columbus,' Mediterranean Squadron, 1840-3: sloop 'Vandalia,' Home Squadron, 1843-5: Naval School, 1846.

Promoted to Passed Midshipman, July 11, 1846: attached to steamer 'Spitfire,' Home Squadron, 1846-7. Was in the several attacks on Vera Cruz; on board the 'Spitfire' when that vessel, assisted by two other gunboats, captured a ten-gun fort a few miles below Tabasco: in several skirmishes in and about Tabasco: at capture of Tuspan and Tampico; frigate 'Brandywine.' Brazil Squadron, 1847-8; razee 'Independence,' Mediterranean Squadron, 1849-52: Coast Survey, 1853: sloop 'Dale' Coast of Africa, 1854-5.

Promoted to Master, 1855. Commissioned as Lieutenant, September 16 [14], 1855; sloop 'Jamestown,' Coast of Africa, 1856, receiving-ship, Boston, 1857-9: store-ship 'Release,' Brazil Squadron, 1860-61: Navy Yard, Portsmouth, N. H., 1862-3.

Commissioned as Lieutenant-Commander, July 16, 1862: commanding steamer 'Nipsic,' South Atlantic Blockading Squadron, 1863. In November, 1863, was appointed Fleet-Captain of the South Atlantic Squadron, and served in that capacity until June 25, 1865; was a number of times under fire at Charleston and

Stono Inlet; Navy Yard, Portsmouth, N. H., 1866.

Commissioned as Commander, July 25, 1866; commanding steam-sloop 'Resaca,' North Pacific Squadron, 1867-8; ordnance duty, Navy Yard, Boston, 1869.

[Retired 1872—see above.] Promoted to Captain [Retired list], 1872. Died April 14, 1872."

Hamersly's Naval Records, 1890.

Brewster, John W.—4th N. H.

"Corporal, Co. B. Residence, Portsmouth. Date of Muster, Sept. 18, 1861, for 3 years. Promoted to Sergeant. Wounded slightly, Oct. 22, 1862. Promoted to 2d Lieutenant, Co. B. Date of Commission, Dec. 1, 1862. Wounded May 20, 1864. Discharged for disability, Sept. 14, 1864."

Adjutant General's Records, N. H.

Briggs, Francis—U. S. Navy.

Brown, Chas. H.—1st N. H. H. Art.

"Corporal, 1st Co., H. Art., N. H. Volunteers, afterwards Co. A., 1st N. H. H. Art. Residence, Lisbon. Date of Muster, May 26, 1863, for 3 years. Promoted to Sergeant November 14, 1864. Mustered out September 11, 1865."

Adjutant General's Records, N. H.

Brown, George A.—17 Mass. & 1st N. H. H. A.

"Private, Co. F., 17th Mass. Residence Haverhill, Mass. Enlisted April 26, 1861, Date of Muster, July 22, 1861, for 3 years. Promoted to Corporal Nov. 1, 1863. Mustered out August 3, 1864."

Adjutant General's Records, Mass.

"Sergeant, Co. L, 1st N. H. H Art. Residence or assignment, Concord. Ward 6. Date of Muster, Sept 27, 1864, for 1 year. Mustered out June 15, 1865."

Adjutant General's Records, N. H.

Brown, George W.—13th N. H.

"Private, Co. K. Residence or assignment, Newington. Date of Muster, Sept. 20, 1862, for 3 years. Mustered out June 21, 1865. Died at Tilton, N. H., March 5, 1891."

Adjutant General's Records, N. H.

"Born in Nova Scotia. Residence Newington. Died at New Hampshire Soldiers' Home, Tilton, N. H."

Report N. H. Soldiers' Home, 1891-2.

Brown, John W.—13th N. H.

"Private, Co. K. Residence or assignment, Portsmouth. Date of Muster, Sept. 20, 1862, for 3 years. Discharged for disability at Bermuda Hundred, Va., May 20, 1864."

Adjutant General's Records, N. H.

Brown, Oren P.—10th Mass. Bat.

Enlisted as "Orrin P. Brown."

"Wounded at Ream's Station, Va., Aug 25, 1864; died at Portsmouth, N. H., July 9, 1867." *Stone.*

"Private. Residence, Boston, Ward 9. Enlisted, Dec. 26, 1863. Date of Muster, Dec. 26, 1863, for 3 years. Wounded Aug. 25, 1864. Mustered out June 9, 1865."

Adjutant General's Records, Mass.

Buckley, Michael—U. S. Navy.

Carlton, Joseph W.—U. S. Navy.

"When will parting scenes be o'er,
Separation known no more;
When will friendship bloom again,
Love and bliss forever reign!
When mortality is o'er,
Then will parting be no more.

When will separation cease,
Friendship's sons unite in peace;
Grief no more oppress the heart,
Friends no more be doomed to part!
When the scenes of life are o'er,
Friends will meet to part no more.

When thy virtues we review,
Joys departed spent with you;
Hope renews the pleasing strain,
Surely we shall meet again.
Yes! when this frail body dies,
We shall meet beyond the skies."

Stone.

Carter, Henry M.—16th N. H.

"Died at New Orleans. . . . He sleeps in Southern soil." *Stone.*

"Private, Co. K. Residence or assignment, Portsmouth. Date of Muster, Oct. 29, 1862, for 9 months. Died of disease at New Orleans, La., June 21, 1863."

Adjutant General's Records, N. H.

Case, Heman—1st Me. H. Art.

Member Storer Post, G. A. R.

"Private, Co. L. Born in Lubec, Maine. Resident of Lubec, Maine. Date of Muster, Jan. 1, 1864, for 3 years. Wounded Aug. 18, 1864. Mustered out and honorably discharged Sept 11, 1865, at Fort Baker, D. C., by reason of orders from War Dept. disbanding Regiment."

Adjutant General's Records, Maine.

"Wounded May 19th 1864, at the battle of Spotsylvania, Va., returned to duty in August, and was again wounded on August 28 [18], 1864, and again returned to duty with his regiment December 1. 1864. . . . Mustered out at Washington, D. C. Sept 11, 1865."

Soldiers Memorial, 1887.

Caswell, Charles R.—13th N. H.

"Private, Co. K. Residence or assignment, Rye. Date of Muster, Sept. 20, 1862, for 3 years. Discharged for disability at Washington, D. C., Dec. 11, 1862."
Adjutant General's Records, N. H.

Caswell, William—8 Inf. & 1 Bat. Mass., & 1 U. S. Vet.

"Private, Co. D., 8th Mass. Infantry. Residence, Lynn. Enlisted ——. Date of Muster, April 30, 1861, for 3 months. Discharged Aug. 1, 1861, expiration of service.

Private, 1st Mass. Battery. Residence Boston. Enlisted Aug 28, 1861, for 3 years. Date of Muster ——. Discharged Aug. 29, 1864, expiration of service.

Private, U. S. Veteran Volunteers (Hancock Corps). Residence North Chelsea, Mass. Enlisted Jan. 17, 1865. Date of Muster ——. Discharged Jan. 6, 1866."
Adjutant General's Records, Mass.

Chace, Horace J.—U. S. Navy.

"Son of Asahel P. and Grace Chace. Died at Indian River, Fla. . . . Buried at sea."
Stone.

Chamberlain, Albert Jr.—U.S.Navy.

Chase, Algernon F.—2nd N. H.

"Enlisted in Co. B, 2nd Reg. N. H. V., Aug. 9, 1862. . . . Died Aug. 27, 1862."
Stone.

"Private, Co. B. Recruit. Residence, Somersworth. Date of Muster, Aug. 12, 1862, for 3 years. Died of disease Aug. 27, 1862."
Adjutant General's Records, N. H.

Clark, Augustus L.—U. S. Navy.

"Augustus Leroy Clark," son of "C. A. & V. L. Clark."
Stone.

Clark, Charles H.—U. S. N. & 1st N. H. H. Art.

Served on U. S. Steamer "R. R. Cuyler" and other vessels while in the U. S. Navy.

"Private, Co. K. 1st N. H. H. Art. Residence or assignment, Portsmouth, Ward 1. Date of Muster, Sept. 17, 1864, for 1 year. Mustered out June 15, 1865."
Adjutant General's Records, N. H.

Clark, George—Mass. Vols.

"A soldier in Mass. Infantry, 1861-1865."
Stone.

Clark, George H.—7th Mass. & U. S. M. C.

Enlisted as "George Clark."
Member S orer Post, G. A. R.

"Private, Co. E, 7th Mass. Residence Dorchester, Mass. Enlisted May 14, 1861. Date of Muster, June 15, 1861, for 3 years. Mustered out June 27, 1864."
Adjutant General's Records, Mass.

"Private, U. S. M. C. Birthplace England. Enlisted Dec. 27, 1864. Promoted to Corporal. Discharged Dec. 28, 1868, expiration of service."
Post Records.

Clark, Thomas K.—26th Mass.

"Private, Co. C. Residence Pepperell, Mass. Enlisted Dec. 12, 1863. Date of Muster, Dec. 12, 1863, for 3 years. Mustered out Aug. 26, 1865, as absent sick. (Discharged May 25, 1865.)"
Adjutant General's Records, Mass.

Clough, Nathan—13th N. H.

"Private, Co. K. Residence or assignment, Rye. Date of Muster, Sept. 20, 1862, for 3 years. Mustered out May 12, 1865. Died at Rye, N. H., January 14, 1872."
Adjutant General's Records, N. H.

Coffin, John N.—8 Bat. & 5 V. M. Mass.

"1st Lieutenant, 8th Mass. Battery. Residence Somerville, Mass. Date of Muster, Sept 21, 1862, [see below], for 6 months. Mustered out Nov. 29, 1862.

Captain Co. B. 5th Regiment Mass. Vol. Militia. Residence Somerville, Mass. Date of Muster, July 25, 1864, for 100 days. Discharged as Captain Nov. 16, 1864, expiration of service."
Adjutant General's Records, Mass.

"Born in Portsmouth, March 11, 1825. . . He went to California in '49, and returning took up his residence in Somerville, Mass. He entered the army May 29, 1862, as Lieutenant of the 8th Mass. Battery, and was in the second battle of Bull Run and at Antietam. He afterwards was Captain of the Somerville, Light Infantry in the one hundred days campaign in 1864. During his war service he was frequently commended for his personal bravery. He was for a long time a prominent citizen of Watertown, Mass.; and was a member of Isaac B. Patten Post, No. 81, G. A. R. of that town. He died in Watertown, July 10 [6], 1891, aged 66 years, 4 months."
Soldiers Memorial, 1892.

Colby, John—3d U. S. Art.

Cole, Edwin O.—1st Me. H. Art.

"Private, Co. L. Born in Skowhegan, Maine. Resident of Guilford, Maine. Date of Muster, Dec. 31, 1863, for 3 years. Mustered out and honorably discharged Sept. 11, 1865, at Fort Baker, D. C., by reason of orders from War Dept. disbanding Regiment."

Adjutant General's Records, Maine.

Cole, Levi W.—4th N. H. & U. S. N.

"Lost at sea near the Georges Banks." *Stone.*

"Private, Co. H, 4th N. H. Recruit. Residence Newcastle, N. H. Date of Muster, Dec. 24, 1863, for 3 years. Transferred to U. S. Navy, April 28, 1864, as ordinary seaman. Served on U. S. Steamers 'Mackinaw' and 'Tioga.' Discharged at New York city, Nov. 17, 1865."

Adjutant General's Records, N. H.

Collins, John—10th N. H.

"An honest man." *Stone.*

"Private, Co. G. Residence or assignment, Greenland. Date of Muster, Sept. 12, 1862, for 3 years. Mustered out June 21, 1865."

Adjutant General's Records, N. H.

Collins, Joseph—U. S. Navy.

Conners, John—U. S. Navy.

Connor, Benjamin—Rev. War.

"Benjamin Connor,
a Revolutionary Officer.
Born
in Exeter, N. H.,
April 8, 1748.
Departed this life
at Greenland, N. H.,
Dec. 29, 1835.
Blessed are the dead who die
in the Lord." *Stone.*

"In September, 1776, the General Court of New Hampshire voted to reinforce the army at New York with two regiments, the first of which was placed under the command of Colonel Thomas Tash. Captain Daniel Gordon's company of this regiment contained the following officers and men belonging to Exeter. . . . [Men] . . . Benjamin Conner."

Bell's History of Exeter.

Cox, George—U. S. Navy.

"Born in England. Residence, Portsmouth. He enlisted in the U. S. Navy, at Portsmouth, April 17, 1862, for 3 years, as 2nd class fireman, served on the U. S. Steamers 'Mahaska' and 'Nipsic,' and April 22, 1865, received an honorable discharge from the U. S. naval service."

Soldiers Memorial, 1892.

Critchley, Thomas H.—13th N. H.

Enlisted as "Thomas Critchley."
Member Storer Post, G. A. R.

"Died May 3, 1885 [1886]." *Stone.*

"Private, Co. K. Residence or assignment, Portsmouth. Date of Muster, Sept. 20, 1862, for 3 years. Transferred to Band, 3rd Brigade, Getty's Division, 18th Army Corps, January 21, 1863. Mustered out, Richmond, June 21, 1865, as 2nd class Musician, as of Band, 2nd Brigade, 3rd Division, 24th Army Corps."

Adjutant General's Records, N. H.

"Birthplace, England." *Post Records.*

Crowley, Michael—U. S. Navy.

Cunningham, Bernard—U. S. Navy.

Currier, Willie H.—3rd U. S. Art.

Curtis, Charles H.—13th N. H.

"1st Lieut., Co. C. Residence Farmington. Commissioned, Sept. 27, 1862. Promoted to Captain, Co. F. Date of Commission, Oct. 28, 1864. Mustered out, June 21, 1865. Died in North Cambridge, Mass., March 19, 1891."

Adjutant General's Records, N. H.

Daily, Milo H.—11th Mass. Bat.

"Killed June 19, 1864." *Stone.*

"Private. Residence Cambridge, Mass. Enlisted——. Date of Muster, Aug. 25, 1862, for 9 months. Discharged May 25, 1863, expiration of service. Reënlisted in same Battery as Private, Jan. 4, 1864. Residence, Cambridge, Mass., Ward 3. Date of Muster, Jan. 6, 1864, for 3 years. Killed in action at Petersburg, Va., June 19, 1864."

Adjutant General's Records, Mass.

Danielson, Fred.—U. S. Navy.

Danielson, Joseph H. — 13th N. H.

Enlisted as "Joseph N. Danielson."

"J. N. Danielson." *Stone.*

"Corporal, Co. K. Residence or assignment, Portsmouth. Date of Muster, Sept. 20, 1862, for 3 years. Discharged for disability at Philadelphia, Pa., Jan. 12, 1863."

Adjutant General's Records, N. H.

David, George E.—13th N. H.

Davidson, James—13th N. H.

"Private, Co. K. Residence or assignment, Portsmouth. Date of Muster, Sept. 20, 1862, for 3 years. Promoted to Corporal. Discharged for disability at Portsmouth, Va., Oct. 7, 1863."

Adjutant General's Records, N. H.

Davidson, James—U. S. Art. & N. H. Vols.

"Captain, Unattached Company N. H. Volunteers, stationed at Fort Constitution, Portsmouth Harbor, N. H. Residence, Newcastle. Date of Muster, May 15, 1862. No record of muster out at Adjutant General's office, Washington. The enlisted men of this company were transferred to Co. E, 9th Reg. N. H. Vols., Aug. 23, 1862 [and Captain Davidson was then probably mustered out].

Adjutant General's Records, N. H.

Davis, Alfred E.—6th N. H.

Davis, Lewis—10th N. H.

Same stone with Thomas J. Davis, 13th N. H.

Lewis and Thomas J. Davis.

"Sweet sleep the Brave who sunk to rest,
With all their country's wishes blest:
Their names survive with honor rare,
And patriots' tears their praise declare."

Stone.

"Private, Co. G. Residence or assignment, Portsmouth. Date of Muster, Sept. 4, 1862, for 3 years. Discharged for disability Jan. 12, 1863."

Adjutant General's Records, N. H.

Davis, Thomas J.—13th N. H.

Same stone with Lewis Davis, 10th N.H.

"Died June 14, 1864." *Stone.*

"Private, Co. C. Residence or assignment, Newcastle. Date of Muster, Sept. 19, 1862, for 3 years. Killed near Petersburg, Va., June 15 [see above], 1864."

Adjutant General's Records, N. H.

Dearborn, George E.—U. S. Navy.

Member Storer Post, G. A. R.

"Birthplace, Effingham; residence, Greenland. Enlisted Sept. 6, 1864. Second class fireman on U. S. S. 'Colorado.' Discharged Sept. 7, 1867, expiration of term of service."

Soldiers Memorial, 1890.

Dearborn, Samuel D.—8th N. H.

"Private, Co. I. Residence or assignment, Middleton. Date of Muster, Dec. 20, 1861, for 3 years. Transferred to Co. G., 20th Invalid Corps, Feb. 16, 1864. Discharged for disability April 18, 1864."

Adjutant General's Records, N. H.

Dennett, George F.—19th Mass.

Enlisted as "George Dennett."

"George Franklin Dennett,
member of 19th Mass. Regt.
Died at Andersonville, Ga.,
Sept. 4, 1864, Aged 33 yrs."

Stone.

"Private, Co. E. Residence Boston, 4th District. Enlisted May 30, 1864. Date of Muster, May 30, 1864, for 3 years. Captured. Mustered out June 30, 1865, as absent—prisoner [see above]."

Adjutant General's Records, Mass.

Dennett, Robert O.—U. S. Navy.

"Acting Third Assistant Engineer, 17 December, 1862. Acting Second Assistant Engineer, 1 February, 1864. Appointment revoked (Sick), 10 October, 1864."

Hamersly's General Navy Register.

Dennett, Thomas S.—U. S. Vols.

"Capt. Thomas Sims Dennett . . . Died at New Orleans, La." *Stone.*

"Appointed from Massachusetts. Captain, Assistant Quartermaster of Volunteers, 30 June, 1862. Discharged 18 July, 1863."

Hamersly's Regular Army Register.

Denny, John—U. S. Navy.

DeWit, Carsten B.—U. S. Navy.

Yeoman of the U. S. Steamer "Kearsarge" when she destroyed the "Alabama," off Cherbourg, France, June 19, 1864. See record of Mark G. Ham.

Dimick, Justin—U. S. Army.

"General
Justin Dimick.
United States Army.
Born
August 6, 1800.
Died
October 13, 1871.
Graduated at the Military Academy
July 1st, 1819. Served as an officer of
Artillery through all the grades from
Second Lieutenant to Colonel.
Was brevetted Major for 'gallant and
meritorious conduct' in the Florida
War, Lieutenant Colonel and Colonel
for 'gallant and meritorious conduct'
in the Mexican War, and Brigadier
General for 'long, gallant and
faithful services to his country.'
An earnest Christian Soldier, ever

faithful to his family, his country and his God."

Stone.

"Born in Connecticut. Appointed a Cadet at the U. S. Military Academy, from Vermont, in 1814. Graduated."

"2nd Lieut., Light Artillery, 1 July, 1819. Transferred to 1st Artillery, 1 June, 1821. 1st Lieut., 1 May, 1824. Captain, 6 April, 1835. Major, 1 April, 1850. Lieut. Colonel, 2nd Artillery, 5 Oct., 1857. Colonel, 1st Artillery, 26 Oct., 1861. Retired 1 Aug., 1863. Died 13 Oct., 1871.

Brevet Rank:—Brevet Captain, 1 May, 1831, for ten years faithful service in one grade. Brevet Major, 8 May, 1836, for gallant and meritorious conduct in the war against Florida Indians. Brevet Lieut. Colonel, 20 Aug. 1847, for gallant and meritorious conduct at Contreras and Churubusco. Brevet Colonel, 13 Sept., 1847, for gallant and meritorious conduct at Chapultepec. Brevet Brigadier General, 13 March, 1865, for long, gallant and faithful services to his country."

Hamersly's Regular Army Register.

"Dimick, Justin, soldier, born in Hartford county, Conn., 5 [6] Aug., 1800; died in Philadelphia, Pa., 13 Oct., 1871. He was graduated at the U. S. Military Academy in 1819, and assigned to the Light Artillery. After serving at various posts, and as assistant instructor of infantry tactics at West Point for a few months in 1822, he was promoted to 1st Lieutenant in the 1st Artillery, 1 May, 1824, and brevetted Captain, 1 May, 1834, for ten years faithful service in one grade.

He was given his full commission in 1835, and brevetted Major, 8 May, 1836, for gallant conduct in the Florida war, having on that date killed two Seminole Indians in personal encounter while skirmishing near Hernandez plantation. He was engaged in suppressing the Canada border disturbances at Rouse's Point, N. Y., in 1838-9, and in the performance of his duty seized a vessel laden with ammunition for the Canadian insurgents. For this act he was called upon in 1851-3 to defend a civil suit in the Vermont courts.

He served as Lieut Colonel of an Artillery battalion of the army of occupation in Texas in 1845-6, and during the Mexican war received two brevets, that of Lieutenant-Colonel, 20 Aug., 1847, for gallantry at Contreras and Churubusco, and that of Colonel on 13 Sept., for his services at the storming of Chapultepec, where he was wounded. Besides these battles, he was at Resaca de la Palma, La Hoya, and the capture of the city of Mexico.

He served again against Florida Indians in 1849-50 and 1856-7, was made Major in the 1st Artillery, 1 April, 1850, Lieutenant-Colonel 5 Oct., 1857, and commanded the Fort Monroe artillery school in 1859-61.

He was promoted to Colonel on 26 Oct., 1861, and commanded the depot of prisoners of war at Fort Warren, Mass., until 1 Jan., 1864. He was retired from active service on 1 Aug., 1863, and in 1864-8 was Governor of the Soldiers' Home near Washington, D. C. On 13 March, 1865, he was brevetted Brigadier-General, U. S. Army, 'for long, gallant, and faithful services to his country.'"

Appleton's Cyclopædia of American Biography.

Dimick, Justin E.—2nd U. S. Art.

"Lieutenant
Justin E. Dimick,
son of Col. Justin
and Mary C. Dimick,
was mortally wounded at
the Battle of Chancellorsville on 3rd May while in
command of Battery H. 2nd
Reg. U. S. Artillery, & died on
5th May, 1863. Aged 23 y'rs.
He was a gallant Officer, a dutiful Son
and an affectionate Brother."

Stone.

"Born in New Hampshire. Appointed a Cadet at the U. S. Military Academy, at Large, in 1856. Graduated."

"2nd Lieut. 6th Infantry, 24 June, 1861. 1st Lieut., 24 June, 1861. Transferred to 1st Artillery, 14 Aug., 1861. Died 5 May, 1863, of wounds received at the Battle of Chancellorsvile, Va. [3 May, 1863]."

Hamersly's Regular Army Register.

Dixon, John—U. S. Navy.

Downing, Havillah F.—Mex. War & 6th N. H.

"Havilah F. Downing." *Stone.*

"Corporal, Co. C, 9th U. S. Infantry, Mexican War. Residence, Portsmouth. Enlisted March 25, 1847, to serve during the war."

Adjutant General's Report, N. H. 1868.

"Private, Co. H, 6th N. H. Residence, Portsmouth. Date of Muster, Nov. 28, 1861, for 3 years. Reënlisted Jan. 4, 1864. Private, Co. H. Residence or assignment, Portsmouth. Date of Muster, Jan. 4, 1864, for 3 years. Mustered out July 17, 1865."

Adjutant General's Records, N. H.

Downing, John—U. S. Navy.

Downing, Nelson N.—U. S. Navy.

"Son of Nelson N. and Caroline W.

Downing. . . . He passed to the spirit world while gallantly defending the flag of his country from on board the U. S. Steamer Pensacola, Apr. 24, 1862, in the bombardment of Forts Jackson and Phillips, New Orleans Harbor.

Rest faithful boy, rest
Thy work is done;
We shall meet thee soon again."

Stone.

"Upon recommendation of the President.

A resolution of thanks to Captain David G. Farragut, of the United States Navy, and to the officers and men under his command.

That the thanks of the people and of the Congress of the United States are due and are hereby tendered to Captain David G. Farragut, of the United States Navy, and to the officers and men under his command, composing his squadron in the Gulf of Mexico, for their successful operations on the lower Mississippi river, and for their gallantry displayed in the capture of Forts Jackson and St. Philip, and the city of New Orleans, and in the destruction of the enemy's gunboats and armed flotilla.

Sec 2. And be it further resolved, That the Secretary of the Navy be directed to communicate this resolution to Captain Farragut, and through him to the officers and men under his command.

Approved July 11, 1862."

Hamersly's General Navy Register.

Drew, Charles H.—22nd Mass. & U. S. N.

"Private, Co. I, 22nd Mass. Residence, Boston. Enlisted Sept. 6, 1861. Date of Muster, Sept. 6, 1861, for 3 years. Discharged Oct. 3, 1862, for disability.

2nd Class Fireman, U. S. Navy. Born in Troy, N. Y. Residence or assignment, Southampton, Mass. Enlisted at Boston, Dec. 7, 1864, for 3 years. Served on U. S. Steamer, 'Wando.' Discharged from U. S. receiving ship 'Princeton,' March 28, 1865."

Adjutant General's Records, Mass.

Drew, Isaac C.—16th N. H.

"Private, Co K. Residence or assignment, Portsmouth. Date of Muster, Oct. 25, 1862, for 9 months. Discharged to date, Aug. 20, 1863."

Adjutant General's Records, N. H.

Driver, Robert—18th Mass.

"Private, Co. B. Residence, Portsmouth, N. H. Enlisted Aug. 20, 1861. Date of Muster, Aug. 24, 1861, for 3 years. Prisoner of war, May 5, 1864. Mustered out Sept. 2, 1864."

Adjutant General's Records, Mass.

Dunn, Clarence—19th Mass.

"Son of Joshua and Caroline W. Dunn. Died at Fair Oaks." *Stone.*

"Died at camp at Fair Oaks, Virginia."

Portsmouth Chronicle, July 4, 1862.

"Private, Co. D. Residence, Boston. Enlisted Aug. 21, 1861. Date of Muster, Aug. 28, 1861, for 3 years. Died of disease at Fair Oaks, Va., June 21, 1862."

Adjutant General's Records, Mass.

Edney, Charles A.—16th N. H.

Enlisted as 'Charles H. Edny."

"Son of George P. and Mary W. Edny, died Aug. 24, 1863, aged 18 years. . . . God's young Patriot." *Stone.*

"Musician, Co. K. Residence, Portsmouth. Date of Muster, Oct. 25, 1862, for 9 months. Mustered out Aug. 20, 1863 [Died Aug. 24, 1863]."

Adjutant General's Records, N. H.

Edney, George A.—89th N. Y.

Emery, James H.—16th N. H.

"1st Sergeant, Co. K. Residence or assignment, Portsmouth. Date of Muster, Oct. 25, 1862, for 9 months. Reduced to Private, May 16, 1863. Mustered out Aug. 20, 1863."

Adjutant General's Records, N. H.

Eugen, Peter—U. S. Navy.

Member Storer Post, G. A. R.

"Birthplace, Norway; residence, Portsmouth. . . . Enlisted February 14, 1865, in the U. S. Navy. Discharged November 22, 1867, by order of the Bureau of Equipment and Recruiting."

Soldiers Memorial, 1891.

"Seaman, U. S. Ship 'Vandalia' "

Post Records.

Evans, Acanthus G.—U. S. Navy.

"Boy. Birthplace, Portsmouth, 1848. Enlisted Nov. 14, 1862, U. S. Steamer 'Ossipee.' Rated Landsman. Discharged Dec. 6, 1864, expiration of service."

Post Records.

Fall, Edwin H.—32nd Mass.

"Son of Otis and Elizabeth Fall. . . . Killed at the battle of Gettysburg. . . . A good son and a brave soldier." *Stone.*

"Private, Co. I. Residence, Charlestown, Mass. Enlisted Aug. 6, 1862. Date of Muster, Aug. 11, 1862, for 3 years. Killed at Gettysburg, Penn., July 2, 1863."

Adjutant General's Records, Mass.

Falvey, John—2nd N. H.

Enlisted as "John Harvey."

"John Falvey. . . . A good Husband, a kind Father." *Stone.*

"Private, Co. K. Residence or assignment, Portsmouth. Date of Muster, June 8, 1861, for 3 years. Discharged for disability, April 21, 1862."

Adjutant General's Records, N. H.

Falvey, Timothy—U. S. M. C.

"Born in Ireland. Residence, Portsmouth. Enlisted October 28, 1859. Discharged March 11, 1865."

Report N. H. Soldiers' Home, 1891-2

Died at New Hampshire Soldiers' Home, Tilton, N. H.

Fishley, George—Rev. War.

"Capt. George Fishley,
died
Dec. 26, 1850,
Aged 91 years."

Stone.

"Deaths. December 26 [1850], Captain George Fishley, aged 90 years and 6 months. Funeral Sunday afternoon [Dec. 29] from St. John's church, immediately after the close of afternoon service [See below].

Capt. Fishley was engaged, during the Revolution, in the service of his country, both upon sea and land. He has long been well known amongst us as a firm patriot and an excellent citizen, and his death will be lamented. Thus one after another the veterans who participated in the struggle for our independence are passing away."

Portsmouth Journal, Dec. 28, 1850.

"Capt. George Fishley. We gave in our paper last week a short obituary of this venerable citizen, who died in this city on the 26th of December [1850], in his 91st year.

Mr. Fishley possessed to the last years of his life, most of his faculties to a remarkable degree. For many years he has on public occasions appeared conspicuously in the processions, in a cocked-hat which almost vied in years with the wearer.

He was born on the 17th day of June, 1760. At the age of seventeen he entered the continental army under Gen. Poor and Col. Dearborn. In the course of the three years of his service he was at the battle of Monmouth [June 28, 1778], (in which action General Washington commanded the American and Sir Henry Clinton the British forces), at the execution of Major André [October 2, 1780], and in the various positions the army occupied at that time. As an instance of revolutionary service, he related that just seventy-three years ago last Tuesday [December 31, 1777], he marched with his companions in arms, several miles, in the vicinity of Valley Forge, without shoes or stockings.

After leaving the land service, he embarked in a privateer on the ocean—was captured, and held as a prisoner at Halifax.

His after life was spent mostly in trading—for many years he had command of a coaster between Portsmouth and Boston—and when by the just provision of a grateful country pensions were granted to the soldiers of the Revolution, he became a recipient of that bounty, and was enabled thereby to descend in comfort to the grave.

In political feelings he was strongly Whig—so much so that when President Polk visited Portsmouth a few years since, he said he declined at first shaking hands with him, because he had no political sympathies with him. In 1840, when the great gathering of the Whigs of New Hampshire was made at Concord, a company of about 300 citizens went from Portsmouth. As an emblem of Commerce, a miniature ship was rigged, and was drawn from our wharves to the political capital of the State. The commander of this vessel, which will be long remembered, was Capt. Fishley.

In 1843 he celebrated his birthday, the 17th of June, in the great meeting on Bunker Hill [held to celebrate the completion of the monument erected in commemoration of the battle fought there sixty-eight years before]. He was among those few Revolutionary soldiers who were companions on that occasion. Incorporated in his very existence was the spirit of '76—and on all fitting occasions it was prominently visible.

With him the last of our cocked hats [and the last veteran of the Revolution residing here, excepting Mark Green and John McClintock] has departed. He was an amiable man, a good citizen, and beloved by all who knew him.

He was buried from St. John's church on Tuesday last—the Portsmouth Greys doing the last military honors to the old patriot."

Portsmouth Journal, January 4, 1851.

George Fishley and Mark Green were the last surviving Revolutionary Soldiers residing in Portsmouth, and took part as such in many Fourth of July and other celebrations.

When President Polk visited Portsmouth July 4, 1847, Fishley and Green, wearing their Continental uniforms and cocked hats, were driven in a carriage in the procession.

It is told of Fishley that when Adams and Jefferson were buried in 1826, and a procession was contemplated in Portsmouth, of which the Revolutionary heroes were to form a part, the committee came to Fishley requesting him to appear. He asked who were to be there. All were named until —— was mentioned. "What" cried the old man, "He a patriot! Why he was a d—— Hessian, and came over here to fight us for six pence a day. No s-i-r, I don't ride with such patriots as he!" And ride he did not on the solemn occasion.

Fitzgerald, Richard—10th N. H.

Member Storer Post, G. A. R.

"Private, Co. G. Residence, Portsmouth. Date of Muster, Sept. 5, 1862. Discharged for disability, Jan. 8, 1864."

Adjutant General's Records, N. H.

"Birthplace, Ireland."

Post Records.

Flynn, John—N. H. Vols.

Ford, James E.—15th N. H. & 1st N. H. H. Art.

Member Storer Post, G. A. R.

"Corporal, Co. F, 15th N. H. Residence or assignment, Danbury. Date of Muster, Oct. 15, 1862, for 9 months. Wounded at Port Hudson, May 27, 1863. Mustered out, Aug. 13, 1863."

Adjutant General's Records, N. H.

"Private, Co. L, 1st N. H. H. Art. Residence or assignment, Concord, Ward 6. Date of Muster, Sept 28, 1864, for 1 year. Promoted to Sergeant. Mustered out June 15, 1865."

Adjutant General's Report, N. H., 1866.

"Birthplace, Orange, N. H."

Post Records.

Foss, Robert S.—13th N. H.

"Private, Co. K. Residence or assignment, Rye. Date of Muster, Sept 20, 1862, for 3 years. Mustered out June 21, 1865."

Adjutant General's Records, N. H.

Foster, Robert F.—23rd Mass.

"Private, Co. C. Residence Boston. Enlisted Sept. 1, 1861. Date of Muster, Sept. 28, 1861, for 3 years. Discharged by order of War Department, Oct. 13, 1864."

Adjutant General's Records, Mass.

Foye, John Harrison—13th N. H.

Enlisted as "John H. Foye."

"Son of Nathaniel G. and Martha L. Foye, died at Suffolk, Va."

"Here rests a son and brother brave
Who in his country's darkest hour
His precious life most nobly gave,
To save it from rebellion's power."

Stone.

"Private, Co. E. Residence, Rye. Date of Muster, Sept. 30, 1862. Killed at Suffolk, Va., May 3, 1863."

Adjutant General's Records, N. H.

"John H. Foye, a member of Co. E, 13th N. H,, was the first Rye man killed in battle during the civil war. This was at the siege of Suffolk, Va., in May, 1863; his body was brought home after the war, and interred in the Foye family burying ground at Rye."

Portsmouth Daily Eve. Times, June 3, 1892.

Foye, Thomas F.—War 1812.

Franklin, Fred A.—3rd Md.

"He served three years and was honorably discharged. He was not sent to the front with his regiment, but was detailed for hospital service in Baltimore.

Family Records.

Franklin, Fred. H.—U. S. Navy.

"Frederick Henry, son of F. A. and Mary Abby Franklin." *Stone.*

He enlisted as "James Barnes," and was a seaman on the U. S. S. "Colorado" at the capture of Fort Fisher. After the war he reënlisted as "Frederick Franklin," and was a quartermaster on the U. S. S. "Colorado" in June, 1871, receiving a medal of honor for his services in Corea at that time.

"General Order, No. 169,

Navy Department.
February 8, 1872.

Medals of honor are hereby awarded to the following named seamen and marines, who have distinguished themselves in battle, or by extraordinary heroism in the line of their profession:

In the attack on and capture of the Corean forts, June 11, 1871.

* * * * * * * *

Frederick Franklin, quartermaster, U. S. S. 'Colorado,' who assumed command of Company D after Lieutenant McKee was wounded, and handled it with great credit till relieved.

* * * * * * * *

GEO. M. ROBESON,
Secretary of the Navy."

Freeland, John—17th N. H.

"Died in camp at Concord, N. H."

Stone.

"Private, Co. B. Residence, Pelham. Date of Muster, Nov. 13, 1862, for 9 months. Died of disease in camp at Concord, N. H., January 16, 1863."

Adjutant General's Records, N. H.

Fretson, Richard—U. S. Navy.

Fuller, Theodore—War 1812.

Gammon, James T.—2nd N. H.

"Private, Co. K. Residence or assignment, Portsmouth. Date of Muster, June 8, 1861, for 3 years. Wounded at Bull Run, Va., Aug. 29, 1862. Captured at Gettysburg, Pa., July 2, 1863. Released. Reënlisted, Private, Co. K. Residence or assignment, Portsmouth. Date of Muster, Jan. 1, 1864, for 3 years. Promoted to Corporal, June 1, 1864. Wounded at Cold Harbor, Va., June 4, 1864. Discharged for disability at Concord, N. H., May 20, 1865."

Adjutant General's Records, N. H.

"Born in Portsmouth, N. H., October 13, 1842. Enlisted at Portsmouth, May 21, 1861, in Co. K, 2nd Regiment, N. H. Infantry. . . . Reënlisted in the same company on June 1, 1864 [See above]. . . . Discharged from the service May 20, 1865, on account of wounds. He participated in most of the battles in which the 2nd N. H. Regiment was engaged, some of which were: First and second Bull Run, Antietam, Fredericksburg, Gettysburg, Cold Harbor, and a great many other engagements. He was wounded in the head at the second battle of Bull Run, August 29, 1862, and again in the right hand at Cold Harbor, June 3 [4], 1864. He was also taken prisoner at the battle of Gettysburg, July 2, 1863. . . . He died June 28, 1887, at his residence in this city."

Soldiers Memorial, 1888.

He was a member of Storer Post, G. A. R., under its first charter.

Gannon, Thomas—2nd N. H.

"Private, Co. K. Residence, Portsmouth. Date of Muster, June 8, 1861, for 3 years. Wounded at Bull Run, Va., Aug. 29, 1862. Mustered out June 21, 1864."

Adjutant General's Records, N. H.

Gardner, Franklin E.—10th N. H.

"Son of Capt. Joseph and Louisa M. Gardner." *Stone.*

"Private, Co. G. Residence, Portsmouth. Date of Muster, Sept. 4, 1862, for 3 years. Died at West Philadelphia, Pa., Feb. 3, 1863."

Adjutant General's Records, N. H.

Gardner, William—Rev. War.

"To
the memory of
William Gardner.
An honest man,
a friend to the Church,
and a sincere liberal
Patriot.
Died April 29, 1834.
Aged 83."

Stone.

A tablet, with similar inscription, will be found in St. John's church, Portsmouth.

William Gardner was Ensign of Capt. John Langdon's company of Cavalry, which volunteered for, and took part in General Sullivan's campaign in Rhode Island, in the summer of 1778.

"William Gardner was of Portsmouth, born in 1751, and bred a merchant, becoming a successful and wealthy one. He was one of the leading patriots of the town of Portsmouth, in word and deed. Being agent for clothing for the United States, he received a requisition for blankets, when there were none in Portsmouth market, and no money in his hands, and still worse, the government had little credit.

Learning that a merchant of Newburyport had a supply of them, Major Gardner repaired to that town to purchase, but was refused them on the credit of the government. He purchased them on private account, and gave his own note for them. The requisition was filled, the soldiers supplied, but when the note became due, Major Gardner had to pay it from his own funds, very much to his own inconvenience, if not injury. In after years he presented his claim to a bankrupt treasury in vain.

He was appointed 'U. S. Loan officer' by Washington, as some remuneration for his sacrifices. I am not aware that he held any other military office than the present one [see above],—which gave him the title of Major, as by the order of the Committee of Safety, empowering Capt. John Langdon to raise an independent company in Portsmouth, he was to rank as colonel, and of course, his lieutenant and ensign, as lieutenant colonel and major. Major Gardner continued as U. S. Loan Officer as long as the office was continued. He died April 29, 1833 [1834], in the 83d year of his age."

Adj. General's Report, N. H. Vol. 2, 1866.

"Died. In this town, on Tuesday last [April 29, 1834], William Gardner, Esq., aged 83 years;—he held the office of Commissioner of Loans for many years:—was one of the most venerable and respectable of our citizens:—one, distinguished for the integrity of his life, the honesty of his heart, and the purity of his motives:—one of the most warm and faithful patriots of his country;—one of the most generous friends to the cause of humanity; one, remarkable for courteousness of manners, true hospitality, disinterested, active and ardent benevolence, and his domestic virtues. Precious is his memory to his friends and fellow citizens.

His funeral, we understand, will be this afternoon, at three o'clock, from his late dwelling house."

Portsmouth Journal, May 3, 1834.

Gates, Storer H.—1st N. H. Cav.

Enlisted as "Story H. Gates."

Member Storer Post, G. A. R.

"Private, Troop A. Residence or assignment, Lebanon. Date of Muster, March 10, 1864, for 3 years. Promoted to Sergeant May 1, 1864. Mustered out July 15, 1865."

Adjutant General's Records, N. H.

"Birthplace, Lebanon, N. H."

Post Records.

Gates, Warren G.—3rd N. H.

"Died at Morris Island, S. C."

Stone.

"Private, Co. D. Residence or assignment, Portsmouth. Date of Muster, Aug. 23, 1861, for 3 years. Died of disease at Morris Island, S. C., Nov. 20, 1863."

Adjutant General's Records, N. H.

Gay, Thomas S.—U. S. Navy.

"Thomas S. Gay,
died Mar. 29, 1886,
Aged 49 yrs.
A gallant officer of the U. S. Navy
in the War of the Rebellion, and
was prominent in the Expedition
which destroyed the Confederate
Ram Albermale, October 28, 1864."

Stone.

"Mate, 30 March, 1864. Acting Ensign, 27 October, 1864. Honorably discharged 1 November, 1868. Sailmaker, 6 December, 1871. Resigned 3 March, 1873."

Hamersly's General Navy Register.

"A resolution tendering the thanks of Congress to Lieutenant William B. Cushing, of the United States Navy, and to the officers and men who assisted him in his gallant and perilous achievement in destroying the rebel steamer Albemarle, in compliance with the President's recommendation to Congress of the 5th of December, 1864.

That the thanks of Congress are due, and are hereby tendered, to Lieutenant William B. Cushing, of the United States Navy, and to the officers and men under his command, for the skill and gallantry exhibited by them in the destruction of the rebel iron-clad steamer Albemarle, at Plymouth, North Carolina, on the night of the 27th of October, 1864.

Approved December 20, 1864."

Hamersly's General Navy Register.

Gerrish, George A.—1st N. H. Bat.

"Captain. Residence, Portsmouth. Commissioned Sept. 10, 1861. Captured, Groveton Pike, Va., Aug. 29, 1862. Paroled. Wounded, Fredericksburg, Dec. 13, 1862. Honorably discharged March 7, 1863."

Adjutant General's Records, N. H.

The 1st N. H. Battery left Manchester, N. H., where it was recruited and organized, November 1, 1861, and proceeded to Washington, D. C.

After various services, on August 29, 1862, the day before the second battle of Bull Run, the Battery took part in a reconnoissance on the Warrenton road toward Groveton, Va. The command met the enemy and suffered severely. The Battery lost several men killed and wounded. "Captain Gerrish, with ten men, was captured by the enemy."

Captain Gerrish was held as a prisoner of war (at Richmond); but was soon exchanged and rejoined the Battery at Upperville, Va., in November, 1862.

The Battery took part in the battle of Fredericksburg December 13, 1862. "Captain Gerrish, then acting Chief of Artillery of the First Division, was wounded early in the action, and taken from the field."

"On the 8th [7th] of March [1863], Captain Gerrish being still disabled by his wound, resigned his commission."

Adjutant General's Reports, N. H., 1865 and 1866.

"Death of Captain Gerrish.—Capt. George A. Gerrish, formerly commander of the First New Hampshire Battery, who was severely wounded at the battle of Gettysburg [Fredericksburg], while acting as Chief of Artillery of the First Division of the Army, died on Saturday [Sept. 1, 1866], at his residence in Chelsea, Mass., from the effects of his wound. His funeral took place Monday afternoon at 2 o'clock, from the Universalist church, under the charge of the Masonic fraternity of which he was a member. His age was 32."

Portsmouth Journal, Sept. 8, 1866.

Gilpatrick, Reuben E.—5th N. H.

Member Storer Post, G. A. R.

"Private, Co. D. Residence, Dover. Date of Muster, Oct. 26, 1861, for 3 years. Wounded at Antietam, Md., Sept. 17, 1862. Wounded at Gettysburg, Pa., July 1863. Discharged for disability Jan. 1, 1864."

Adjutant General's Records, N. H.

"Birthplace, Dover, N. H. Gunshot wounds in shoulder and left hand at Antietam, Sept. 17, 1862; in left shoulder through to lung and left forefinger at Gettysburg, July 2, 1863."

Post Records.

Goodrich, Edwin R.—2nd N. H. & U. S. Vols.

"First Lieutenant, Co. K, 2nd N. H. Residence or assignment unknown. Date of commission, June 20, 1861 Promoted to Commissary Subsistence, U. S. Vols., October 31, 1861. Resigned January 7. 1865."

Adjutant General's Records. N. H.

"Appointed Captain, Commissary Subsistence, of Volunteers, 31 October, 1861, from New York. Resigned, 7 January, 1865."

Hamersly's Regular Army Register.

"Born in Portsmouth, in January, 1826. He learned the printer's trade in this city and in Boston: afterwards engaging in business in New York. He entered the service at the outbreak of the Rebellion, enlisting for three months in the 7th New York Regiment [See below]. Later he joined the 2nd New Hampshire Regiment, with a commission as First Lieutenant and Quartermaster, June 20th, 1861. In the following October he was made Captain and Commissary of Subsistence on the staff of General Burnside, and all through the perilous and glorious career of the 9th army corps he was in charge of its means of sustenance. He was frequently called upon for service under fire as aide-de-camp, and had numerous narrow escapes.

In July, 1862, he was promoted to Lieutenant Colonel: in March, 1865, he was brevetted Colonel, and in April, 1865, Brigadier General, for meritorious service. With characteristic modesty, however, he preferred the lesser title of Colonel, for it was in that rank that he did actual service.

After the rebellion he served for two years on the staff of Gov. Fenton, of New York, and in that capacity was stationed at Washington in charge of the adjustment of the war accounts between that state and the general government. In all this long and responsible service his patriotism and his integrity won the recognition of his superiors, and no accusation of personal interest or profit was ever laid at his doors.

At the conclusion of this duty he went to Brooklyn, N. Y., to reside, and while there his attractive home and fine library were entirely destroyed by fire, causing him great financial loss, from which he never recovered.

In person Col. Goodrich had a commanding figure, and his thick mass of snow-white hair and beard made him a notably dignified figure. He was a fine conversationalist.

Died April 22, 1892, in Boston, aged 66 years 3 months."

Soldiers Memorial, 1892.

The Record and Pension office of the War Department states that "the name of Edwin R. Goodrich has not been found on the rolls of any company of the 7th New York State Militia, of 1861, on file in this [that] office."

Goodrich, J. Nelson—U. S. Navy.

Appointed as "Nelson Goodrich."
Member Storer Post, G. A. R.
"J. N. Goodrich, U. S. Navy."

Stone.

"Birthplace, Portsmouth. Appointed Boatswain, U. S. Navy, July, 1861. Resigned January, 1863."

Post Records.

Boatswain. Born in New Hampshire and appointed from New Hampshire. He was Boatswain of the U. S. Steamer "Pensacola," August 31, 1861, and September 1, 1862, as shown by the Navy Registers of those dates, and was attached to the "Pensacola" in that capacity at the passage of the Forts and the capture of New Orleans by Farragut, April 23 and 24, 1862.

His name does not appear in the Navy Register of January 1, 1863, nor in "Hamersly's General Navy Register."

Goodrich, Marco B.—4th Cal.

"Marco Bozzaris Goodrich." *Stone.*

"Private, Co. D. Date of Muster, Sept. 21, 1861, at Volcano, California, for 3 years. Honorably discharged October 15, 1864, at Fort Vancouver, Washington Territory, by reason of expiration of term of service."

Adjutant General's Records, Cal.

Goodwin, Ichabod—War Governor, N. H.

"Ichabod Goodwin,
Died on the Fourth of July, 1882,
Aged Eighty-Seven Yrs.
He was Governor of New Hampshire
from June 1859 to June 1861,
including the first months
of the War of the Rebellion."

Stone.

"The death of Ex-Governor Ichabod Goodwin occurred at his residence on Islington street, on the evening of July 4th [1882], at 8.45 o'clock, and was not wholly unexpected, as he had been confined to his bed and in a precarious condition for several weeks past.

Ex-Governor Goodwin was born in North Berwick, Me., October 1794, and was the eldest son of Samuel Goodwin. At the age of fourteen he entered the counting room of Samuel Lord, Esq., merchant, of this city, and in 1817 went to sea as supercargo of ship Elizabeth Wilson, in the employment of J. P. and Samuel Lord. Not many months after he sailed as master and supercargo of one of the ships of this firm and became interested with them in the vessels he commanded. In 1832 he engaged in an extensive mercantile business in connection with Samuel E. Coues, Esq., in this city, and never thereafter went to sea.

He represented this city in the New Hampshire Legislature in 1838,43,44,50, 54, and '56, and was a member of the Constitutional Convention in 1850 and 1876. He was first President of the Eastern Railroad Company in New Hampshire, and held the office for twenty years. In 1847 he was elected President of the Portland, Saco and Portsmouth Railroad Company, which office he held for a long term of years, until 1871, we think. He was also first President of the Portsmouth Steam Factory, in whose success he always manifested the liveliest interest. In 1857 the degree of master of arts was conferred on him by Dartmouth college.

In March 1859 Mr. Goodwin was elected Governor of New Hampshire, and was reëlected in 1860, his term of office extending to June 5th, 1861, covering the breaking out of the rebellion and the raising of the first two regiments of volunteer infantry from this State. This was a most trying period in the history of New Hampshire, and nobly and patriotically did the Governor meet the emergency. The people everywhere had confidence in his wisdom and financial skill, and when he issued a call for men and money for the war, they responded promptly. There then being no funds in the treasury aside from what was required to meet the ordinary expenses of the state, and the crisis demanding that the quota of men called for by the President. from New Hampshire, should be raised and made ready for the field without delay. he personally appealed to the banking institutions and private individuals of the State for assistance, and they promptly placed at his disposal six hundred and eighty thousand dollars.

To call an extra sesion of the Legislature would involve not only delay but expense, and Governor Goodwin, with the advice of his council, assumed the entire responsibility as commander-in-chief of the militia to act without special legislative authority. The result of his work became, as we all know, a vital part of our State's history. On the assembling of the Legislature in June, Gov. Goodwin plainly and concisely stated the position he assumed and the motives which actuated him. The Legislature at once endorsed all his acts by unanimously passing the enabling act, relieving the Governor of his heavy responsiblity. His administration of State affairs for two years met with almost universal approval, and he left the office with the highest respect of all parties.

Because of an earnest desire to retire from the active duties of life, ex Governor Goodwin had been gradually withdrawing from official positions, but at the time of his death he was President of the following organizations:—First National Bank, Piscataqua Savings Bank, Portsmouth Gas Company, Portsmouth Bridge Company, and Portsmouth Howard Benevolent Society, which offices he held with ability.

As a member of the Legislature and of the Constitutional Convention he took a leading part on committees and in debate. His speeches were never made for show: he spoke only when there seemed to be occasion for it, and then always to the point, and was listened to with great respect and attention, for his conservatism and practical wisdom in all matters of public policy were well-known.

In 1827 he married Sarah Parker Rice, daughter of William Rice, Esq., a wealthy merchant in this city, by whom he had seven children: his wife, one son and two daughters surviving him.

His last appearance before the public was on the evening of Memorial day, May 30, 1882, in Music Hall, at which (as in all the years since that day was set apart for remembering the dead heroes of the late war) the ex-Governor presided, and as usual gave an address full of patriotic sentiment. His remarks on that occasion were particularly choice and delivered with unusual force.

Without neglecting any private duty, he yielded to frequent calls upon his time and services for the public weal, and in everything promotive of the prosperity of his country, state and city, he ever manifested an earnest interest, and every good work found in him an earnest friend and helper.

He was charitable, but his charities were not bestowed 'to be seen of men.'

Very many in this city who have been the recipients of his bounty will miss and mourn a sympathetic friend indeed. In theological opinion he was a Unitarian of the highest type of the Channing school, and was a devoted member of the Stone church in this city. His social life was consistent with the faith he professed, and alike in official or unofficial positions, his influence was helpful to public and private morality. Truly a good man has gone and 'his works follow him.'

What more fitting time for a noble hearted patriot to breathe his last than on the evening of the anniversary of his nation's birthday!

The funeral will take place at the Unitarian church on Saturday [July 8th] at 12 o'clock."

Portsmouth Journal, July 8th, 1882.

Gookin, George E.—24th Mass.

"Died in Boston, Mass." *Stone.*

"Private, Co. H. Residence, Boston. Enlisted July 29, 1862. Date of Muster, July 29, 1862, for 3 years. Discharged Dec. 3, 1864, expiration of service."

Adjutant General's Records, Mass.

Grant, Alexander—Mex. War.

"Private of Company K, 3d U. S. Artillery, died at Fort Constitution, N. H. . . . For fifteen years he nobly supported the honor of his country in the contested fields of Florida and Mexico. This stone was erected by the members of said Company as a tribute of respect to his memory." *Stone.*

Grant, John—War 1812.

Grant, William W.—Mex. War.

"Son of John and Sarah Grant. Died on board of the U. S. Ship Columbus, Monterey." *Stone.*

Gray, Henry D.—1st N. H. H. Art.

"Sergeant, Co. K. Residence or assignment, Portsmouth, Ward 2. Date of Muster, Sept. 17, 1864, for 1 year. Mustered out June 15, 1865."

Adjutant General's Records, N. H.

Green, Mark—Rev. War.

"Mark Green,
a Revolutionary Soldier,
Died Sept. 18, 1851,
Aged 89."

Stone.

"'Soldier in the Fourth Massachusetts Regiment,' from which he was discharged Dec. 31, 1783."

Soldiers Memorial, 1891.

"Deaths. In this city, on Thursday evening last [Sept. 18, 1851], Mr. Mark Green, aged 89.

Mr. Green was three years in the land and sea service of his country in the time of the Revolution. He was an original member of the Mechanics Association, of which he has been a member in good standing for forty-nine years. He was engaged in the building of the first frigate 'Congress.' He has been confined to his house for the present year, but had lost no interest in the scenes, events and remembrances of the Revolution.

At the celebration of the 4th of July the present year [1851], he requested that a portion of the display might pass by his window. The sight afforded him great gratification. The day before his death his thoughts were wandering over his early scenes with such intensity that he remarked, 'Do you hear those guns?—Washington is reviewing his troops!'

The funeral will take place on Saturday afternoon [Sept. 20] at four-o-clock from the residence of Mr. Mark Green, Jr., No. 4 High street. The Mechanics Association will meet at Jefferson Hall at half-past three-o-clock to attend the funeral.

Portsmouth Journal, Sept. 20, 1851.

Thus died and was buried, sixty-eight years after the close of the Revolution, our last resident Continental soldier.

Of the citizens of Portsmouth who took part in the Revolution, Capt. John McClintock, who served in a private-armed vessel, alone survived him.

"Mr. Samuel S. Green, of No. 49 Daniel street, this city, is the son of Mark Wentworth Green, [usually known as Mark Green], who was born in Portsmouth in the year 1762.

He [Mark Wentworth Green] was baptized in Queen's Chapel—now St. John's church—his sponsor being Mark Hunking Wentworth. The interest of the latter gentleman in his godchild took shape in a proposition to send the young man to England to be educated.

Young Green was a patriot, however, and declined the generous offer, and shipped on board a Portsmouth privateer. This vessel was fortunate in capturing three or four prizes, but was in turn captured by three British men-of-war. The youth was sent, a prisoner, to Halifax; but was exchanged not long after, and sent on a cartel to Gloucester, Mass. Like his shipmates, he was penniless, and together they returned on foot to Portsmouth. During the passage from Halifax the men were crowded so closely in the hold of the vessel that no change of position was possible except by command, and 'Ready—About!' was the order by which they were permitted to relieve their cramped bodies.

Upon reaching home Mr. Green enlisted in the federal army and served until the end of the war. With his regiment he witnessed the British evacuation of New York. Upon the disbanding of the patriot army, he, with his comrades from Portsmouth and Eliot, again took the road which led homeward. On arriving at Haverhill they crossed the river on the ice, regardless of danger, so eager were they to reach home and friends.

The father of this young man, Mr. John Green, was carpenter on the privateer 'Rambler' under Paul Jones [See below].

Mr. Samuel S. Green, who counts an experience of seventy years, is justly proud of his patriotic kinsmen, and stands, himself, before his fellow citizens an upright and honorable man, content that in his person his patriotic lineage has suffered no stain."

Portsmouth Daily Chronicle, April 2, 1889.

John Green, stated above to have served on the "privateer 'Rambler' under Paul Jones," is believed by his grandson, Mr. Samuel S. Green, to have sailed from Portsmouth on the "Ranger," Nov., 1, 1777. He was, however, certainly on the U. S. Frigate "Alliance," as the name of "John Green, Carpenter's Mate," appears on the "Roll of the Officers and Crew of the Frigate 'Alliance,' Captain Peter Landais, October 3d, 1779," printed in "Sherburne's Life of John Paul Jones." The "Alliance" was then one of the vessels of Commodore Jones' squadron, and was present when he captured the "Serapis," Sept. 23, 1779, but took little part in the action. Mark Green, not long before his death, received prize money due his father for captures made by the "Alliance."

"Interesting Revolutionary Documents. —Our readers will recall a reference to the services of Mark Green of Portsmouth, in the Revolutionary army and navy, in a recent number of the *Chronicle*. In connection therewith several interesting papers have turned up, the quaintness of which entitles them to a passing notice. Two of them are here presented. The first bears the file-inscription: 'Mark Green's discharge,' and reads thus:

'By the Honorable Major General Knox, commanding the American forces on Hudson's River, Mark Green, Soldier in the Fourth Massachusetts Regiment, being inlisted for three years, is hereby honourably discharged from the service of the United States.

Given in the State of New York—the Thirty-first day of December, 1783—

By the General's command

J. Knox, M. Gen.

Registered on the Books of the Regiment. Charles Seldin, Adjutant.

Portsmouth, New Hampshire, April 6th, 1818—I hereby certify that the above discharge is a true copy from the original—

Samuel Fernald, Justice Peace.'

This document is written on half-cap, laid paper, and lines are ruled with a pencil for the convenience of the writer.

The second paper is a printed form, and is thus filed on the middle fold, instead of the outer as is the present custom: 'Mark Green's Pension Certificate. Payable semi-annually. The first payment on this Certificate will be made on the 4th of March next, in Portsmouth, at the U. S. Branch Bank.' At the foot of the fold is the word, 'Recorded.' The document is numbered '16,344.' The body of the instrument reads:

'War Department.
Revolutionary Claim.

I certify that, in conformity with the Law of the United States, of the 18th March, 1818, Mark Green, late a Private in the Army of the Revolution, is inscribed on the Pension List, Roll of the New Hampshire Agency, at the rate of Eight dollars per month, to commence on the Seventh day of April, one thousand eight hundred and Eighteen.

Given at the War office of the United States, this Seventh day of September, one thousand eight hundred and Nineteen. J. C. Calhoun,
Secretary of War.'

To this page is affixed the seal of the War office, stamped on a lozenge-shaped paper over red wax."

Portsmouth Daily Chronicle, April 18, 1889.

Mark Green always made his home in Portsmouth. During his enlistment in the army the encampment for winter quarters was at one time in a large walnut grove on the Hudson river, near West Point. He related that they commenced cutting trees, building huts, and making roads, so that before leaving they had to go a mile or two for their fuel.

Mr. Samuel S. Green is also a nephew of Thomas Harvey, whose Revolutionary service is given on later pages.

Greenough, Robert F.—29th Mass.

"Died at Antietam, Md." *Stone.*

"Private, Co. H. Residence, Charlestown, Mass. Enlisted Nov. 5, 1861. Date of Muster, Nov. 5, 1861, for 3 years. Promoted to Corporal. Killed Sept, 17, 1862."

Adjutant General's Records, Mass.

Griffey, John—U. S. M. C.

Member Storer Post, G. A. R.

"Birthplace, Cumberland, Md.: residence, Portsmouth. . . . Enlisted Nov. 16, 1855, as Private in U. S. M. C. Discharged Nov. 16, 1860. Reenlisted Nov. 16, 1860. Placed on the retired list, U. S. M. C., Jan. 20, 1888, on account of being in the service 30 years. . . . Served 32 years, 1 month, and 20 days."

Soldiers Memorial, 1890.

"Discharged from U. S. M. C. as Private, Jan. 20, 1887 [See above]."

Post Records.

Gunnison, Nathaniel—13th N. H.

"Son of James B. and Mary Gunnison."

"His fight is fought, the victory won,
His labors all must cease,
For he's gone to camp by a crystal stream,
In the beautiful realms of peace."

Stone.

"Private, Co. K. Residence or assignment, Portsmouth. Date of Muster, Sept. 20, 1862, for 3 years. Died of disease at Portsmouth, N. H., Jan. 10, 1864."

Adjutant General's Records, N. H.

Hadley, Allston W.—U. S. Navy.

"Allston Wentworth Hadley."

Stone.

Hahir, James—10th & 2nd N. H.

Ham, Henry E.—30th Me., & U. S. Navy.

"Son of J. E. and Julia A. Ham. . . . Died at Acapulco. . . . Yeoman, U. S. Ship Resaca.—Served three years as Commissary Sergeant of 30th Regt. Maine Veterans."

See below. *Stone.*

"Private, Co. E. 30th Maine. Born in Waldoboro, Maine. Resident of Portsmouth, N. H. Date of Muster, August 1, 1863, for 3 years. Appointed Commissary Sergeant 30th Maine, January 9, 1864. Reduced to Private April 16, 1864. Mustered out and honorably discharged August 20, 1865, at Savannah, Georgia, by reason of orders from War Dept., disbanding Regiment."

Adjutant General's Records, Maine.

Ham, Mark G.—U. S. Navy.

"Mark G. Ham,
died
March 11, 1869,
Aged 51.
Carpenter U. S. S. 'Kearsarge,'
at the sinking of the 'Alabama,'
June 9, 1864."

Stone.

The Alabama was captured June 19, and not June 9, 1864.—See below.

"Mark G. Ham, carpenter's mate, Kearsarge" was one of the sixteen men of the crew of the "Kearsarge" to whom "medals of honor" were awarded by the Navy Department.

Navy Department G. O. No. 45, Dec. 31, 1864.

"Carpenter's Mate on board of the U. S. Steamer 'Kearsarge' when she destroyed the 'Alabama' off Cherbourg, France, June 19, 1864. 'Exhibited marked coolness and good conduct, and is highly commended by his Divisional Officer.'"

Record of the Medals of Honor issued to the Blue Jackets and Marines of the United States Navy, 1862—1877. Washington, 1878.

"A resolution tendering the thanks of Congress to Captain John A. Winslow, United States Navy, and to the officers and men under his command, on board the United States steamer Kearsarge, in her conflict with the piratical craft the Alabama, in compliance with the President's recommendation to Congress of the 5th of December, 1864.

That the thanks of Congress are due, and are hereby tendered, to Captain John A. Winslow, of the United States Navy, and to the officers, petty officers, seamen and marines of the United States steamer Kearsarge, for the skill and gallantry exhibited by him and the officers and men under his command in the brilliant action on the 19th of June, 1864, between that ship and the piratical craft Alabama, a vessel superior to his own in tonnage, in guns, and in number of her crew.

Approved, December 20, 1864."

Hamersly's General Navy Register.

The following named men, who were on board the "Kearsarge" when she destroyed the "Alabama," are buried in or near Portsmouth:

Barnes, William A.—Landsman—St. Mary's.

DeWit, Carsten B.—Yeoman—Newington.

Ham, Mark G.—Carpenter's Mate—Harmony Grove.

Salmon, Thomas—2d Class Fireman—Calvary.

Smart, George E.—2d Class Fireman—Harmony Grove.

Hamilton, John—5th & 27th Me.

"Private, Co. F, 5th Maine. Born in Rollingsford, Maine [Rollinsford, N. H.]. Resident of Kittery, Maine. Date of Muster, June 24, 1861, for 3 years. Honorably discharged Sept. 4, 1861, by reason of disability.

Corporal, Co. G. 27th Maine. Reënlisted. Date of Muster, Sept. 30, 1862, for 9 months. Honorably discharged March 18, 1863, at Camp General Casey by reason of disability."

Adjutant General's Records, Maine.

Hammond, Pierpoint—10th N. H.

"Private, Co. G. Residence or assignment, Portsmouth. Date of Muster, Sept. 4, 1862, for 3 years.

Absent sick in Hospital at Portsmouth Grove, R. I. Died at Portsmouth, N. H., Sept. —, 1864."

Adjutant General's Records, N. H.

Hanson, Frank B.—44th Mass.

"Died at Newbern, N. C." *Stone.*

"Private, Co. A. Residence, Boston. Enlisted ——. Date of Muster, Sept. 12, 1862, for 9 months. Died at Newbern, N. C., June 11, 1863."

Adjutant General's Records, Mass.

Hanson, John K. A.—13th N. H.

"Private, Co. K. Residence or assignment, Portsmouth. Date of Muster, Sept. 20, 1862, for 3 years. Captured at Fredericksburg, Va., Dec. 13, 1862. Released, May 20, 1863. Mustered out June 21, 1865."

Adjutant General's Records, N. H.

Harding, Samuel Jr.—U. S. Navy.

"Died at Brooklyn, N. Y." *Stone.*

Harmon, John—13th N. H.

"Private Co. K. Residence or assignment, Portsmouth. Date of Muster, Sept. 20, 1862, for 3 years. Captured at Fredericksburg, Va., Dec. 13, 1862. Released, May 20, 1863. Wounded slightly, Sept. 29, 1864. Mustered out June 21, 1865."

Adjutant General's Records, N. H.

Harmon, Luther—4th N. H.

"Died at Morris Island, S. C."

Stone.

"Private, Co. B. Residence or assignment, Portsmouth. Date of Muster, Sept. 18, 1861, for 3 years. Promoted to Corporal. Died of disease at Morris Island, S. C., Dec. 23, 1863."

Adjutant General's Records, N. H.

Harris, John—U. S. M. C.

Hartnett, John—U. S. Navy.

"A native of the parish Balenspittle, Co. Cork, Ireland." *Stone.*

Harvey, Thomas—Rev. War.

"Thomas Harvey,
a worthy
Soldier of the Revolution,
Died
Jan. 18, 1837,
Aged 84 years."

Stone.

"Deaths.—In this town, Mr. Thomas Harvey, aged 85 [See above]—a Revolutionary pensioner."

Portsmouth Journal, January 21, 1837.

"We announced the death a week or two since of Thomas Harvey, a Revolutionary pensioner, at the age of 85 [See above]. The following incident is related in a Boston paper:

'When Lafayette visited Portsmouth in 1824 an interesting scene occurred in the hall of audience. Harvey was introduced to the General as a soldier who had fought under him. 'Do you recollect, Marquis (said Harvey), who bore you on his back, after being wounded at the battle of Brandywine, to the surgeon's quarters?' 'He was called Tom Harvey,' said the excellent Lafayette. What took place thereafter, if we know, it is not proper to relate.'"

Portsmouth Journal, February 4, 1837.

Thomas Harvey was born in Portsmouth in 1752 or 1753, and served gallantly in the Continental army during seven years of the Revolutionary war. He crossed the Delaware with Washington, and was at the battle of Brandywine, Sept. 11, 1777. He died in Portsmouth, January 18, 1837.

When Lafayette visited Portsmouth, Wednesday, September 1, 1824, and was given a public reception in Franklin Hall, at least thirty soldiers of the Revolution, who had served under him, and many of whom had come from a great distance for the purpose of seeing him, were present.

Among those who pressed forward to shake hands with the illustrious visitor was Thomas Harvey. While retaining the General's hand the veteran asked him if he remembered who carried him off the field severely wounded at the battle of Brandywine?

"I do," instantly replied the General—"It was a New Hampshire soldier named Thomas Harvey, who rendered me that gallant service."

"Yes," said the soldier, "It was Thomas Harvey, and—with a military salute—I am the man."

The General recognized his friend of the battle-field, and manifested great pleasure at meeting him again after the lapse of so many eventful years, and greeted him with a cordiality and a warmth of manner highly gratifying to the patriot soldier.

A newspaper of the time says: "Our old friend Thomas Harvey found it difficult to restrain himself; the sight of Lafayette recalled all the scenes of the Revolution and well nigh overcame him."

Harvey was always very patriotic and could ill brook a Tory, as was a citizen of Portsmouth, whose hired man he was for a time. The story is told, that one morning he was with him at the old Spring Market, with his basket, when Governor Langdon came in with his hired man and basket. Mr. Harvey's employer said to him—"Why can I not have my shoes shine like Governor Langdon's?" The reply was—"Because he is a gentleman!"—"And am I not a gentleman?"—The answer was—"No!"—with a capital N so forcibly given, that a sympathizing citizen, standing near, put half a dollar in Harvey's hand.

In his later years Harvey was not overburdened with this world's goods, and was bent nearly double, but he received a small pension, and was always happy and contented, and quick witted also, as the following incident will show.

The Benevolent Society of the then town of Portsmouth had a committee appointed to visit the poor one hard winter to ascertain their wants.

Among others Mr. Harvey was visited, and the gentleman apologized for his visit, by saying—"You look very comfortable here, I am a sort of a spy going around"—Harvey interrupted him excitedly by saying,—"I don't like spies, we hung one (André) in the Army, and a handsome man he was too! A good deal better looking than you are!"

Haselton, Geo. Ed.— . . . .

"Killed in battle at Savage Station, Va."

Stone.

Haven, Nathaniel A.—Rev. War.

Nathaniel Appleton Haven.

"Hon.
Nathaniel A. Haven,
Died
March 13, A. D. 1831,
Aged 69 years.
Blessed are the dead
who die in the Lord."

Stone.

Nathaniel A. Haven was born in Portsmouth in 1762, graduated at Harvard College in 1779, was several years a physician, and afterwards a merchant of Portsmouth, and Member of Congress in 1809.

He was the son of Rev. Samuel Haven, D. D., fifty-four years pastor of the South Church in Portsmouth: who was born August 4, 1727, in Framingham, Mass., graduated at Harvard College in 1749, ordained minister of the South Church, Portsmouth, May 6, 1752, received the degree of Doctor in Divinity from the University of Edinburgh in 1770, and afterward from Dartmouth College, and died March 3, 1806, aged 79.

Nathaniel A. Haven was Assistant Surgeon, or Surgeon, of an armed vessel in the latter part of the Revolutionary war. The vessel was captured by the British, and he was confined as a prisoner of war on board the Jersey prison ship at New York, but was soon exchanged at the special request of General Washington.

Haven, N. Parker—Phil. City Cav.

Enlisted as "Nathan P. Haven"

"Son of William and Susan P. Haven. . . . Died in New York." *Stone.*

"Private, Capt. Thomas C. James' Co., 1st Troop. Enrolled April 29, 1861, to serve 3 months. Mustered out August 17, 1861."

War Department Records.

Haven, S. Cushman—162nd N. Y.

Samuel Cushman Haven was son of James Henderson and Elizabeth (Cushman) Haven, and grandson of Hon. Samuel Cushman, all of Portsmouth, where he himself passed several years of his boyhood. A flag, with wreath and flowers, has for many years been placed on Memorial Day near his grandfather's stone in Proprietors' cemetery, Portsmouth, in remembrance of him: but he is buried in the National Cemetery at Baton Rouge, Louisiana, where friends, who became greatly attached to him at New Orleans a few months before his death, have erected a stone to his memory, inscribed with his name and age, the passage,

"Blessed are the pure in heart, for they shall see God," and beneath it the stanza from Longfellow,—

"He, the young and strong, who cherished
Noble longings for the strife,
By the roadside fell and perished,
Weary with the march of life."

"2nd Lieutenant, Co. B. Enrolled Sept. 15, 1862. Commissioned 2nd Lieutenant, Dec 3, 1862, with rank from Sept. 20, 1862. Died June 25, 1863, at Baton Rouge, Louisiana, of diptheria."

Adjutant General's Records, N. Y.

"Samuel Cushman Haven was born in Nauvoo, Ill. [where his parents temporarily resided], Feb. 19, 1843."

He graduated at Harvard College in

1862. "He had hoped to become a physician, but postponed his studies to serve his country, and immediately after graduation was commissioned as Second Lieutenant in the 162nd Regiment N. Y. Volunteer Militia [N. Y. Volunteers] under General Banks.

In February 1863, he was promoted to a first-lieutenancy [See below]. On the 15th of June he was obliged to leave his regiment, then before Port Hudson, to go to the hospital at Baton Rouge where he died of diptheria on the 25th of June, 1863."

The Adjutant of the Regiment wrote to a member of Mr. Haven's family from "Before Port Hudson, June 27, 1863," as follows:

"Colonel Benedict desires me to say that the 162nd Regiment has, in his opinion, lost one of its very best and most faithful officers, one whom he had recommended for promotion, and whose place cannot be filled. The late Lieutenant Haven's conduct as an officer and bearing as a gentleman have, ever since the formation of the regiment, met the Colonel's unqualified approval. He begs you to assure his friends that he sympathizes with them in the grief his loss will excite."

Class Book, Class of 1862, Harvard, 1882.

"From the records of this office it does not appear that Samuel C. Haven, a 2d Lieut. of Co. B, 162 N. Y. V., was ever promoted to 1st Lieut."

Letter from Adjutant General, New York.

An extended notice of Lieutenant Haven by Rev. Andrew P. Peabody, D. D., will be found in "Harvard Memorial Biographies." Volume II, Cambridge, 1866.

Hazlett, William C.—U. S. Navy.

Heheir, Thomas W.—U. S. Navy

Henderson, George D.—U. S. Navy.

George Donald Henderson.

"Chaplain, 2 July, 1864. Died 20 May, 1875."

Hamersly's General Navy Register

"Died at Portsmouth, N. H., May 20, 1875." *Navy Register, 1876.*

Hennessey, Daniel—U. S. Navy.

Hewins, Otis W.—10th N. H.

"Private, Co. G. Residence or assignment, Portsmouth. Date of Muster, Sept. 4, 1862, for 3 years. Promoted to Sergeant. Reduced to Private Dec. 1, 1862. Discharged for disability Nov. 11, 1863."

Adjutant General's Records, N. H.

Hill, Alfred J.—Mex. War & 3rd N. H.

Member Storer Post, G. A. R.

"Sergeant, Co. C, 9th U. S. Infantry, Mexican War. Residence, Portsmouth. Enlisted March 2, 1847, to serve during the war."

Adjutant General's Report, N. H., 1868.

"Adjutant, 3rd N. H. Residence, Portsmouth. Commissioned, August 7, 1861. Resigned April 14, 1862."

Adjutant General's Records, N. H.

"Birthplace, Durham, N. H."

Post Records.

Hill, John Edward—19th Mass.

"Son of Daniel and Elizabeth Hill. . . . Died at Georgetown, D. C., Sept. 11, 1862, from wounds received near Fairfax Court House, Va., while discharging his duty as Surgeon of the 19th Regt. Mass. Vols. . . . Strangers closed his dying eyes." *Stone.*

"Asst. Surgeon. Residence, Charlestown, Mass. Date of Commission, July 24, 1862. Died of wounds, Sept 11, 1862."

Adjutant General's Records, Mass.

Hodgdon, George E.—10th N. H. & V. R. C.

Member Storer Post, G. A. R.

"First Lieutenant, Co. G, 10th N. H. Residence or assignment, Portsmouth. Date of Commission, Sept. 18, 1862. Resigned Feb. 14, 1863."

Adjutant General's Records, N. H.

"To be Second Lieutenant, in the Veteran Reserve Corps, George E. Hodgdon, to date from April 30, 1864."

General Orders No 256, War Dept., A. G. O., Sept. 15, 1864

"Birthplace, Barnstead, N. H.; residence Portsmouth; occupation lawyer. Enlisted September 5, 1862, as private in Co. G, 10th N. H. Volunteers. Commissioned First Lieutenant September 18, 1862. Resigned February 14, 1863. Commissioned January 2, 1864 [See above], as Second Lieutenant Veteran Reserve Corps. Detailed on staff duty as Aide de Camp and Judge Advocate. Resigned, as Captain Veteran Reserve Corps, March 29, 1866."

"In civil life he was honored with the highest offices of his city, serving as City Solicitor, Alderman, member of the Board of Education, member of the Legislature in 1875, 1887-'88-'89-'90-'91, and Mayor of Portsmouth in 1888 and 1889. In 1889 he took the lead in the House of Representatives in favor of the establishment of the N. H. Soldiers' Home, and to him is largely due its success in that body.

On the reorganization of Storer Post, No. 1. of Portsmouth, he became a member [June 28, 1878], was elected its commander in 1880, and since then has been an earnest worker and prominent leader in the ranks of the Grand Army.

In 1885 he served as Assistant Adjutant-General, Judge Advocate in 1887, Junior Vice Department Commander in 1889, Senior Vice Department Commander in 1890, to both the latter positions being unanimously chosen, and had he not absolutely refused further preferment he would have been chosen Department Commander at the last state encampment [1891], his business engagements and health warning him not to take upon himself the labors and responsibilities of the office. He was undemonstrative in his nature, but firm in his convictions, and had hosts of warm personal friends, especially among his comrades."

"Died in Portsmouth, June 11, 1891. Age 52 years."

Soldiers Memorial, 1892.

Mr Hodgdon was much interested in our local history, and contributed to the *Portsmouth Journal* some interesting and valuable "Annotations" on "Adams' Annals of Portsmouth."

Hodgdon, Harland P.—10th N. H. & I. C.

Enlisted as "Harlan P. Hodgdon."

"Private, Co. G. Residence or assignment, Portsmouth. Date of Muster, Sept. 1, 1862, for 3 years. Promoted to Corporal. Transferred to 28th Co., 2nd Batt. Invalid Corps, Aug. 13, 1863. Discharged at Portsmouth, N. H., July 19, 1865."

Adjutant General's Records, N. H.

Hodgdon, Henry C.—13th N. H.

"Private, Co. K. Residence or assignment, Portsmouth. Date of Muster, Sept. 20, 1862, for 3 years. Died of disease at New York City, Dec. 23, 1862."

Adjutant General's Records, N. H.

Hodgdon, William C.—War 1812.

"Private, Capt. Jacob Dearborn's Company, 3rd Regiment, N. H. Detached Militia, Edward Sise, Lieut-Colonel Commandant. Residence, Newington. Enlisted Sept. 26, 1814, for 60 days."

Adjutant General's Report, N. H., 1868.

Stationed at Fort Washington, Portsmouth Harbor, N. H.

A large force of the N. H. Militia was called out by Governor J. T. Gilman, in September, 1814, for the defense of Portsmouth.

"The British had made every arrangement to destroy the Navy Yard and the town of Portsmouth. For this purpose their cruisers were off the bay of Piscataqua. A British officer told Col. Walbach, after the war, that he went up the Piscataqua and reconnoitred the town, disguised as a fisherman, and returned to the fleet and reported that the town was swarming with soldiers and well defended: and the British commander abandoned the project of attacking the town."

"The danger being past, the British forces evidently extended their predatory warfare southward. The main part of the troops, detached for the protection of Portsmouth, were discharged about the 1st of October. A small detachment of troops still remained, however, until winter approached."

Adjutant General's Report, N. H., 1868.

Holbrook, John A.—U. S. Navy.

"Sailmaker, 3 January, 1862. Died 2 January, 1866."

Hamersly's General Navy Register.

"Died at Portsmouth, N. H., January 2, 1866." *Navy Register, 1867.*

Hook, William S.—14th Maine.

"Private, Co. ——. Recruit. Born in Canada. Served on quota of Buxton, Maine. Date of Muster, March 25, 1865, for 3 years. Mustered out and honorably discharged, May 11, 1865, at Galloup's Island, Boston Harbor, Mass., by reason of orders of War Dept. reducing the Army."

Adjutant General's Records, Maine.

Hough, Andrew J.—U. S. Navy.

"Carpenter, 30 August, 1861. Died 2 September, 1861."

Hamersly's General Navy Register.

Howard, Ferd. M.—Mass. Vols.

The regiment is entered incorrectly as "6th N. H. Inf.," on his stone. He is believed to have been in a Massachusetts regiment, but which one is not known.

Hoyt, Franklin C.—Mex. War.

Hunter, Hugh—U. S. Navy.

"Seaman. Birthplace, Portsmouth, 1839. Enlisted Dec. 16, 1860, U. S. Ship 'Macedonian.' Discharged Dec. 29, 1863. Reënlisted, Seaman, U. S. Ship 'New Hampshire' May 20, 1864. Discharged March 6, 1867, expiration of service,"

Post Records.

He is said to have served on the "Congress," "Pensacola," and "Nahant."

When he was attached to the Monitor

"Nahant," during one of the attacks on the forts at Charleston, S. C., orders were given to change projectiles; and it became necessary to withdraw a cartridge after it had been placed in the XV inch gun, in order to substitute a larger or smaller one. Is was impossible to withdraw it quickly, in the usual manner, and to save time Hunter crawled into the heated gun and drew out the cartridge, so that the gun was reloaded and ready to fire when the turret had completed its revolution and the gun bore again upon the enemy.

Huntress, Charles E.—2nd N. H.

"Private, Co. K. Residence or assignment, Portsmouth. Date of Muster, June 8, 1861, for 3 years. Died of disease at Alexandria, Va., Sept. 20, 1862."

Adjutant General's Records, N. H.

Huntress, Seth— 4th N. H.

Enlisted as "Seth W. Huntress."

"Private, Co. B. Residence, Portsmouth. Date of Muster, Sept. 18, 1861, for 3 years. Discharged to date Sept. 27, 1864."

Adjutant General's Records, N. H.

Jackson, Hall—Rev. War.

"In memory of
Hall Jackson, Esquire, M. D.,
Who departed this life
On the 28th of Sept., 1797,
Ætat 58

To heal disease, to calm the widow's sigh,
And wipe the tear from poverty's swollen eye;
Was thine! but ah! that skill on others shown,
Tho' life to them, could not preserve thy own:
Yet still thou liv'st in many a grateful breast,
And works like thine enthrone thee with the blest."

Stone.

Dr. Hall Jackson was born in Hampton, N. H., Nov. 11, 1739. [His father, Dr. Clement Jackson, removed from Hampton to Portsmouth about 1749.]

Hampton Church Records.

"During the Revolution Dr. Hall Jackson was Surgeon in the army, and Captain of an artillery corps."

Portsmouth Guide Book.

"On the 28th of September, 1797, died Dr. Hall Jackson, after a short illness, in the fifty-eighth year of his age. In visiting some patients, his sulkey was overset, whereby several ribs were fractured, and a fever ensued, which terminated his life.

Dr. Jackson was born in this town [See above], and received the first rudiments of his education in the public schools here. He studied the theory of physic and surgery, under the direction of his father, Doctor Clement Jackson. After completing his studies here, he went to London, and attended lectures in the public hospitals there, to perfect himself in surgery. Upon his return to this country, he opened an apothecary's shop, but his practice as a physician soon became so extensive, that he was obliged to relinquish in a great measure, his business as a druggist, and attend almost entirely to his profession.

As a physician, he was skilful; as a surgeon, eminent. No operation of importance was performed for many miles round, without consulting him, and seldom without his aid. He had great experience in the small-pox; and many hospitals, which were established for inoculating with that disorder, were committed to his care, and he was remarkably successful in conducting his patients safely through the disease. In the obstetric art he obtained high reputation, and was frequently applied to for advice and assistance in difficult cases, by persons who did not generally employ him. He frequently performed the operation of couching, and always with success.

Harvard College conferred on him the degree of Doctor of Medicine [1793]; and he was elected an honorary member of the Massachusets Medical Society. He was Grand Master of the Free and Accepted Masons in New Hampshire, at the time of his decease. His sprightly talents, lively imagination, and social habits, rendered him an agreeable companion; facetious and pleasant in conversation, his friends enjoyed in his company 'the feast of reason,' with the flow of wit: and the several societies of which he was a member, found their entertainment greatly heightened by his presence."

Adams' Annals of Portsmouth.

Three letters written by Dr. Hall Jackson, while serving with the Continental army near Boston, dated, "Cambridge, July 19, 1775," "Camp Winter Hill, September 5, 1775," and "Camp on Winter Hill, September 16, 1775," will be found in "Letters by Josiah Bartlett, William Whipple and others, written before and during the Revolution," Philadelphia, 1889. These letters relate to his services in the army.

On Nov. 14, 1775, the Provincial Congress of New Hampshire voted its thanks to Dr. Hall Jackson, and "that he receive a commission from this Congress as Chief Surgeon of the New Hampshire Troops in the Continental Army," as shown by the "Provincial Papers of New Hampshire," Vol. VII, page 657.

In November, 1775, he was Captain of a company of Field Artillery, "stationed in the town of Portsmouth, upon the

Parade," and in September, 1776, he was Surgeon of Col. Pierse Long's regiment, as stated in the "Adjutant General's Report, "New Hampshire, Vol. 2, 1866, pages 276 and 290.

Dr. Hall Jackson's residence in 1775, in its present modernized form, is still in existence at the north-east corner of Court and Washington streets, Portsmouth.

Jackson, John H.—Mex. War & 3rd N. H.

"John H. Jackson,
1814—1890.
Col. 3rd N. H. Vols.
Our Hero at rest."

Stone.

"1st Lieutenant, Co. C., 9th U. S. Infantry, Mexican War. Born in New Hampshire. Appointed from New Hampshire. Date of Commission, April 9, 1847. He went out in command of his company . . . and accompanied his regiment on its march to the city of Mexico. He was in all of the battles in the Valley of Mexico, and was brevetted for gallant services on the 19th and 30th [20th] of August, 1847, at the battles of Contreras and Churubusco, and commissioned Captain, February 17, 1848 [See below]. He was mustered out of service at Newport, R. I., in August, 1848."

Adjutant General's Report, N. H., 1868.

"Born in New Hampshire. Appointed from New Hampshire. 1st Lieutenant, 9th [U. S.] Infantry, 9 April, 1847, Captain, 4 December, 1847. Disbanded, 26 August, 1848.

Brevet Rank:—Brevet Captain, 20 August, 1847, for gallant and meritorious conduct at Contreras and Churubusco."

Hamersly's Regular Army Register.

"Lieut. Colonel, 3rd N. H. Residence, Portsmouth. Commissioned, Aug. 6, 1861. Promoted to Colonel. Date of Commission, June 27, 1862. Wounded slightly at Fort Wagner, S. C., July 18, 1863. Honorably discharged for disability, Feb. 24, 1864."

Adjutant General's Records, N. H.

"In Memoriam.
COLONEL JOHN H. JACKSON.
T. E. O. Marvin.

Droop, droop ye banners proud
O'er hero lying low:
Sheathed is his sword, his pennon lowered,
No more the bugles blow.

Hushed is the battle cry;
The tone of stern command—
Bent low in grief o'er fallen chief
His war-worn veterans stand.

Upon his brow they place
The wreath in battle won;
With solemn tread they bear their dead
While booms the minute gun.

No more will Jackson's arm
His battle steed control:
The fight is done, the field is won—
Farewell, intrepid soul.

Let sculptured urn and shaft
Record our hero's name;
Be his the meed of gallant deed,
Undying be his fame."

Portsmouth Penny Post, April 11, 1890.

"Col. John H. Jackson died at his residence in Boston on the 10th April [1890], after a brief illness, at the age of 75 years and 6 months. He was a native of Portsmouth and was the son of John H. Jackson, who died before his birth while nobly fighting in the second war with Great Britain. His grandfather was a soldier in the Revolution, so that the gallant colonel inherited the martial spirit that early in life led him to join the militia and afterward made him the hero of two wars.

He was commissioned April 9, 1847, as First Lieutenant in the 9th U. S. Infantry, for service in the war with Mexico. August 20th of the same year he was brevetted Captain for gallantry in the battles of Contreras and Churubusco, and commissioned as Captain the following December. At the battle of Chapultepec his bravery drew forth honorable mention from his superior officers, and there is no doubt that had the war lasted much longer he would have attained to very high rank. At this battle one of those fortunate occurrences of which we read so often, but which really occur so seldom, happened to the Colonel. While gallantly leading his company in the magnificent charge which resulted in the capture of this hitherto regarded impregnable fortress, he felt himself struck full in the chest by a bullet, but as he found no wound, paid but slight attention to the circumstance until the battle was over, when upon investigation he found that his life had been saved by a pocket bible, the gift of his sister, which was pierced nearly through by a Mexican bullet.

The Colonel was mustered out of the service with his regiment in August, 1848, went to California with the pioneers in 1849, where he remained four years, returning east in 1853, when he was appointed an inspector in the Boston Custom House. He continued to serve in this position until the breaking out of the Rebellion, when he was offered and accepted the commission of Lieutenant-Colonel of the 3rd N. H. Volunteers. The resignation of Col. Fellows promoted him to the command of the regiment June 27, 1862, and he led his men in all their engagements until the storming of Fort Wagner, where he received a severe wound, which incapacitated him from active duty and undoubtedly shortened his life. He was honorably discharged from the service, Feb. 24, 1864. In 1867 he was re-appointed to a lucrative and most important position in the Boston Custom House, and held the place until his decease.

* * *

The following is an extract from a letter of Dec. 9, 1889, from Col. John H. Jackson, dated Custom House, Boston, Mass.:

'My father's family came early to New York from Holland. He was a ship carpenter and served some time in our navy. He had been living at Portsmouth, and early in 1814 he enlisted at Portsmouth, N. H., in Col. Winfield Scott's regiment, and on the 26th of September 1814, at or near Lundy's Lane, he was killed. I was born October 20, 1814, at Portsmouth, N. H. You see I never saw my father. His name was John H. Jackson. No other member of his father's family ever came to Portsmouth.'"

Portsmouth Journal, April 19, 1890.

Jarvis, John B.—N. Y. Vols.

He is said to have served in the 100th N. Y. Regiment of Infantry, but the Adjutant General of New York states that his name is not found on the rolls of any Company of that Regiment.

Jellison, Daniel M.—13th N. H.

"Private, Co. K. Residence or assignment, Portsmouth. Date of Muster, Sept, 20, 1862, for 3 years. Mustered out, May 26, 1865."

Adjutant General's Records, N. H.

Jenkins, William D.—U. S. Navy.

"Died in Flatbush, N. Y." *Stone.*

"Carpenter, 24 March, 1840. Retired list 14 November, 1870."

Hamersly's General Navy Register.

"Died at Flatbush [L. I.], N. Y., April 14, 1883." *Navy Register, 1884.*

Jenness, Albion J.—13th N. H.

"Son of Lowell and Ann L. Jenness. . . . Died at Norfolk, Va. [See below]. . . . A good son, a brave and fearless soldier." *Stone.*

"Private, Co. E. Residence or assignment, Rye. Date of Muster, Sept. 30, 1862, for 3 years. Died of disease at Portsmouth, Va., Aug. 8, 1863."

Adjutant General's Records, N. H.

Jervis, Edward—10th N. H.

Enlisted as "Edward Jarvis."

Member Storer Post, G. A. R.

"Private, Co. G. Residence, Portsmouth. Date of Muster, Sept. 4, 1862, for 3 years. Discharged for disability Dec. 18, 1862."

Adjutant General's Records, N. H.

"Birthplace, England."

Post Records.

Johnson, Abram A.—U. S. Navy.

Member Storer Post, G. A. R.

"Coal Heaver. Birthplace, Portsmouth. Enlisted Nov. 21, 1861, U. S. Steamer 'Brooklyn.' Discharged Oct. 20, 1863. Reënlisted, Coal Heaver, Sept. 2, 1864, U. S. Steamer 'San Jacinto.' Discharged Sept. 23, 1867, expiration of service."

Post Records.

"Mr. Johnson was a veteran of the Rebellion, and served on the flag ship 'Brooklyn,' with Farragut, at the taking of New Orleans, when he was wounded upon the hand by a piece of flying shell."

Portsmouth Daily Evening Post, June 15, 1892.

Johnson, Chas. E.—3rd & 5th N. H.

"Corp'l. C. E. Johnson, Co. D, 3rd N. H. Inf." *Stone.*

"Private, Co. D, 3rd N. H. Residence or assignment, Portsmouth. Date of Muster, Aug. 23, 1861, for 3 years. Discharged for disability at Hilton Head, S. C., Oct. 18, 1862.

Private, Co. C, 5th N. H. Recruit. Residence or assignment, Portsmouth. Date of Muster, Aug. 10, 1863, for 3 years. Mustered out, June 28, 1865."

Adjutant General's Records, N. H.

Jones, Michael—U. S. Navy.

Kane, Dennis—6th N. H.

"Private, Co. H. Residence or assignment, Portsmouth. Date of Muster, Nov. 28, 1861, for 3 years. Discharged for disability at Philadelphia, Pa., Jan. 29, 1863."

Adjutant General's Records, N. H.

Kelenbeck, Christopher—16th N. H. & U. S. N.

Enlisted as "Christopher Kelenberk."

"Private, Co. K, 16th N. H. Residence, Portsmouth. Date of Muster, Nov. 11, 1862, for 9 months. Discharged at New Orleans, March 17, 1863."

Adjutant General's Records, N. H.

Kennard, Nathaniel—Rev. War.

"Sacred
to the memory of
Capt. Nathaniel Kennard,
who departed this life
June 24, 1823,
Aged 68."

Stone.

"Roll of the Officers, Seamen, Marines, and Volunteers, who served on board the 'Bon Homme Richard,' commanded by Commodore John Paul Jones, in her cruise made in 1779."

Name. Rate. Country.
"Nathaniel Kennard.—Boy.—American."

* * * * * * *

The famous action of the "Bon Homme Richard" with, and capture of the "Serapbis," took place on this cruise, Sept. 23, 1779, and all named in this roll were present."

Sherburne's Life of John Paul Jones.

"Died on the 24th inst. [June 24, 1823], Capt. Nathaniel Kennard of this town, aged 68.

His character demands none of the usual unmeaning panegyric of an obituary notice. To those who knew him, his services, his sufferings and his worth will ever render his memory dear. All who partake of the blessings secured by the enterprise and valor of our revolutionary heroes, cannot but feel an interest in the events of his life.

At the commencement of the war of the Revolution, he entered as a volunteer in one of the first regiments in Massachusetts, for the term of one year.

At the expiration of that engagement, he entered on board a private armed vessel—was captured, carried to England and kept in close confinement at the Mill Prison for two years and a quarter, being encouraged with no other prospect than a still protracted confinement, or a termination of it by being hanged as a rebel.

Thence he was sent to France in a cartel, where on the 20th April, 1779, he entered on board the 'Bon Homme Richard,' under the celebrated John Paul Jones, and was with him in some of the most desperate enterprises, in which that commander was engaged. From that vessel he was put on board a prize and ordered for France.

He was again captured and carried into Hull in the north of England, transported to Spithead, put on board the 'Unicorn' frigate and compelled to do duty until at the imminent hazard of his life he escaped in the Island of Jamaica. Thence he returned to America a little before the close of the war.

After the peace of '83 he engaged in the merchant service and continued a reputable shipmaster until near the commencement of the late war [1812-15], when he was appointed by government to the command of a Revenue Cutter and continued in the same to the close of the war.

After that period, until his death, he was employed as Inspector of the Customs at this port. In all his various services, Capt. Kennard sustained the character of an honest man and a good citizen."

Portsmouth Journal, July 5, 1823.

Capt. Nathaniel Kennard was born on Kennard's hill in Eliot, Maine, then a part of Massachusetts, and died in Portsmouth, N. H. His son, Capt. Nathaniel Kennard, Jr., of Portsmouth, was captured in the "Harlequin" privateer in the War of 1812, and afterwards died in the West Indies of yellow-fever.

Kennedy, William—1st Mass. H. Art.

"Private, Co. F. Residence, South Boston, Mass. Enlisted, Aug. 5, 1862. Date of Muster, Aug. 5, 1862, for 3 years. Promoted to Corporal. Mustered out July 8, 1864."

Adjutant General's Records, Mass.

Kennison, William S.—13th N. H.

Enlisted as "William S. Keniston."

"Private, Co. E. Residence or assignment, Newmarket. Date of Muster, Sept. 19, 1862, for 3 years. Discharged for disability at Portsmouth, Va., Sept. 15, 1863."

Adjutant General's Records, N. H.

Kent, John Horace—43rd Mass.

Member Storer Post, G. A. R.

"Private, Co. A. Residence, New Bedford, Mass. Enlisted ——, Date of Muster, Oct. 11, 1862, for 9 months. Promoted to Sergeant. Discharged, July 30, 1863, expiration of service."

Adjutant General's Records, Mass.

"Born in Rochester [Barnstead], N. H., October 10, 1828—died at Concord, N. H., March 4, 1888. . . . When the war broke out he was at Prince Edward's Island." He returned to the United States, "joined Co. A. of the 43rd Regiment of Massachusetts Volunteers, and went to the Department of North Carolina, thence going to the Army of the Potomac. . . . In 1863 he was mustered out, and appointed a special agent of the Provost Marshal's Department for the district of New Hampshire, with headquarters at Portsmouth, holding the office until it was abolished."

Soldiers Memorial, 1888.

"Born in Barnstead, N. H. At the

opening of the Provost Marshal's office in Portsmouth, N. H., he entered that service as a Special Agent and Deputy Provost Marshal, and served until the Provost Marshal's Department was discontinued." *Post Records.*

Storer Post is indebted to his generosity for the series of interesting and valuable war views, and other pictures, which adorn its hall.

Kimball, Chas. H.—17th & 2nd N. H.

"Private, Co. B, 17th N. H. Residence or assignment, Portsmouth. Date of Muster, Nov. 13, 1862, for 9 months. Consolidated with Co. K, 2nd N. H. V., April 16, 1863.

Private, Co. K, 2nd N. H. Recruit. Residence or assignment, Portsmouth. Date of Muster, Nov. 13, 1862, for 9 months. Transferred from 17th N. H. V., April 16, 1863. Mustered out Oct. 9, 1863."

Adjutant General's Records, N. H.

Laighton, Alfred S.—2nd Mass. Cav.

Enlisted as "Alfred Laighton."

"Alfred Seabury, son of Charles E. and Frances S. Laighton. . . . Died at Washington, D. C., July 29, 1863." *Stone.*

"Private, Troop A ["California 100"]. Enlisted in California, Dec. 5, 1862. Date of Muster, Dec. 10, 1862, for 3 years. Died at Hospital, Washington, D. C., July 28 [See above], 1863."

Adjutant General's Records, Mass.

Laighton, Alfred S.—U. S. Navy.

Alfred Stowe Laighton.

"Killed by the explosion at Fort Fisher."

"In man's regret he lives, and woman's tears,
More sacred than in life, and nobler far
For having perished in the front of war."

Stone.

"Acting Ensign, 19 December, 1863. Killed on 'Gettysburg' [See below], 16 January, 1865."

Hamersly's General Navy Register.

He was killed on shore at Fort Fisher, North Carolina, by the explosion which took place the morning after its capture.

Laighton, Bennett—16th N. H.

"Born in Stratham, N. H., Died in Buffalo, N. Y. . . . His life was sacrificed in the war for the preservation of the Union." *Stone.*

"Private, Co. K. Residence or assignment, Stratham. Date of Muster, Oct. 25, 1862, for 9 months. Promoted to Corporal. Died of disease at Buffalo, N. Y., Aug. 20, 1863."

Adjutant General's Records, N. H.

Laighton, William F.—U. S. Navy.

"Thirty years in the U. S. N."

Stone.

"Carpenter, 7 April, 1849. Retired list, 13 November, 1877. Died, 25 June, 1879."

Hamersly's General Navy Register.

"Died at Revere, Mass., June 25, 1879."

Navy Register, 1880.

Laighton, William M.—U. S. Navy.

"Carpenter, 29 September, 1836. Retired list, 15 April, 1872. Died, 23 May, 1873."

Hamersly's General Navy Register.

"Died at Brookline, Mass., May 23, 1873." *Navy Register, 1874.*

Lake, Dayton W.—14th Maine.

"Died at Brooklyn, N. Y." *Stone.*

"Private Co. I. Born in Portsmouth, N. H. Resident of Bangor, Maine. Date of Muster, March 23, 1865, for 1 year. Mustered out and honorably discharged, Aug. 7, 1865, at New York City, N. Y., by reason of orders from War Dept. reducing Army."

Adjutant General's Records, Maine.

Langdon, John—Rev. War.

"Gov. J. Langdon and family."

"John Langdon, born 1739, died Sept. 18, 1819." *Tomb.*

For date of birth see below.

"In memory of
The Honorable
John Langdon, LL. D.
Born 1739—Died 1819.
He was a member of this church
several years.
Erected by
His great grandson,
Alfred Langdon Elwyn,
1890."

Tablet, North Church, Portsmouth.

For date of birth see below.

"In Memoriam.
Honourable John Langdon, LL. D.
Born June 25, 1741. Died Sept. 18, 1819.

Governour Langdon honoured by his presence the Masonic ceremonial at the laying of the corner-stone of this church, June 24, 1807.

Of honest stock: courage and wisdom crowned
The man who still good as he looked was found:
Whom all its honours to his country bound.
Best of the best in his New Hampshire home."

Tablet, St. John's Church, Portsmouth.

"Another mural tablet has been placed in the vestibule of St. John's. It is in memory of the Hon. John Langdon, LL. D., sometime governor of the Province [State] of New Hampshire. The well chosen words of the epitaph inscribed on the monument are largely a translation of those inscribed on the tomb of Scipio Africanus, and were selected for this purpose by the distinguished and scholarly Mr. John Langdon Elwyn [his grandson], now deceased. The monument was erected by the generosity of the Rev. Alfred Langdon Elwyn, of Philadelphia [his great-grandson]."

Portsmouth Daily Eve. Post, Nov. 5, 1891.

"Col. John Langdon was one of the most zealous and worthy patriots of the time, at work in season and out of season, with mind, hands and means, in the cause of liberty. He was born in Portsmouth, in 1740 [See above], and was the son of John, and grandson of Tobias Langdon. He served an apprenticeship as a merchant in the counting-room of the Hon. Daniel Ringe [Rindge], but preferring a sea-faring life, he went out as supercargo of one of Ringe's [Rindge's] vessels and subsequently as master or captain. He continued in this business until the Revolution, and had amassed a handsome fortune for the time. The British cruisers stopping entirely his shipping and mercantile operations, and early espousing the patriot cause, he had inclination, lesiure and means to largely subserve the cause of independence.

He was one of the leaders in taking Fort William and Mary [now Fort Constitution], at Newcastle, in December, 1774, was a Delegate to the general congress in 1775-6, raised an independent company of light infantry, with rank of Colonel, in June of the latter year, was judge of the court of common pleas in 1776, speaker of the House of Representatives in 1776-7, in which last position, during a session of three days, to devise ways and means to check the haughty Burgoyne, he rose at his desk and made the noble, generous, apt and effective speech of the Revolution:—'Gentlemen, I have three thousand dollars in hard money, thirty hogsheads of Tobago rum, worth as much, I can pledge my plate for as much more: these are at the service of the State. With this money we can raise and provision troops, our friend John Stark will lead them. If we check Burgoyne, the State can repay me, and if we do not, the money will be of no use to me.'

Raising the funds and Stark on his way to Bennington, Langdon summoned his own company of infantry and followed to Bennington and Saratoga. Burgoyne defeated, he returned home only to labor in the good cause, and early in 1778, as agent of Congress, built the Raleigh frigate. In this year, also, he mounted his company of infantry, equipped them as cavalry, and marched to the defense of Rhode Island.

In 1779 he was President of the New Hampshire Convention, in 1780 Commissioner of the United States, and in 1783 Delegate to the Congress of the same. In 1784-5, he was a member of the New Hampshire Senate, and in this last year was President of the State, elected as successor of Meshech Weare. In 1788 he was a member of the Convention that formed the Constitution of the United States, was Speaker of the New Hampshire House of Representatives in June of the same year, and was again elected President of the State.

In November of the same year 1788, he was elected to the United States Senate, and had the honor of being elected the first President *pro tem.* of that body, and in 1794, he was reëlected for another term. In 1801 he was elected a representative to the New Hampshire Legislature and was elected for the three successive years, and was Speaker of the House in 1805—when he was elected Governor of the State, and was reëlected to that office until 1809, and again in 1810-11. Col. Langdon died September 18, 1819, aged 79 years.—*D. P. Drown, Jonathan Eastman, John Farmer, and N. H. Rolls.*"

Adjutant General's Report, N. H., Vol. 2, 1866.

"Langdon, John, statesman, born in Portsmouth, N. H., 25 June, 1741, died there, 18 Sept., 1819. After receiving a common-school education he entered a counting-house and became a successful merchant.

In 1774, with John Sullivan and others, he participated in the removal of the armament and military stores from Fort William and Mary [now Fort Constitution] in Portsmouth harbor. He was elected a delegate to the Continental Congress in 1775, but resigned in June, 1776, to become navy agent.

In 1777, while he was speaker of the the New Hampshire assembly, when means were wanted to support a regiment, Langdon gave all his money, pledged his plate, and subscribed the proceeds of seventy hogsheads of tobacco [See above] for the purpose of equipping the brigade with which Gen. John Stark subsequently defeated the Hessians at Bennington. Langdon participated in this battle, and was in command of a volunteer company at Saratoga, and in Rhode Island. In 1779 he was Continental agent in New Hampshire, and president of the State convention.

He was again a delegate to Congress in 1783, was repeatedly a member of the Legislature and its speaker, and in 1787 a delegate to the convention that framed the constitution of the United States.

In March, 1788, he became Governor of New Hampshire, and in 1789 he was elected U. S. Senator, holding office till 1801, and was chosen president of the Senate in order that the electoral votes for President of the United States might be counted [He thus officially announced the election of George Washington as the first President of the United States.] A president of the Senate had therefore a legal existence before there was either a president or a vice-president of the United States.

He was a Republican in politics and acted with Jefferson, who, on assuming office in 1801, offered him the post of Secretary of the Navy, which he declined. From 1805 till 1812, with the exception of two years, he was Governor of New Hampshire, and in 1812 the Republican Congressional caucus offered him the nomination for the office of Vice-President of the United States, which he declined on the score of age and infirmities, passing the remainder of his life in retirement."

Appleton's Cyclopædia of American Biography.

A biography of John Langdon, by his grandson, the late John Langdon Elwyn, of Portsmouth, will be found in Vol. XX. of the "Early State Papers of New Hampshire."

Lear, Nathaniel M.—2nd N. H.

"Private, Co. K. Residence, Portsmouth. Date of Muster, June 8, 1861, for 3 years. Discharged for disability at Washington, D. C., July 31, 1861."

Adjutant General's Records, N. H.

Leary, Jeremiah O.—U. S. M. C.

His stone reads incorrectly—"J. O. Leary, U. S. Navy."

Leary, Timothy O.—16th N. H. & U. S. M. C.

Enlisted as "Timothy O'Leary." Member Storer Post, G. A. R.

"Timothy O. Leary." *Stone.*

"Private, Co. K, 16th N. H. Residence, Portsmouth. Date of Muster, Oct. 25, 1862, for 9 months. Mustered out Aug. 20, 1863."

Adjutant General's Records, N. H.

"Enlisted in U. S. M. C. ——. Discharged from U. S. M. C. Sept. 8, 1868."

Soldiers Memorial, 1890.

"Birthplace, Ireland." *Post Records.*

Leslie, George T.—7th Ill. Cav.

Enlisted as "George T. Brown."

"Private, Troop B. Probable date of death, Nov. 3, 1863."

Letter from Treasury Department.

"Captured. Died at Cahawba Prison, Ala., January, 1863 [1864.] Buried at Cahawba." *Post Records.*

Lester, David G.—War 1812.

"A native of Salisbury, Mass., a soldier of the war of 1812." *Stone.*

Lewis, John C.—1st N. H. & U. S. N.

"Private, Co. B, 1st N. H. Residence, Dover. Date of Muster, May 2, 1861, for 3 months. Mustered out Aug. 9, 1861.

Landsman, U. S. Navy. Residence, Dover. Enlisted, Dec. 12, 1861. Served on U. S. vessels 'Ohio,' 'North Carolina,' 'Princeton,' and 'St. Louis,' Rated Seaman. Discharged from U. S. Ship 'North Carolina,' for disability, August 4, 1863 [See below]."

Adjutant General's Records, N. H.

"Birthplace, New Durham, N. H. . . Enlisted Dec. 12, 1861, as Ordinary Seaman on U. S. Ship 'Constellation,' from which ship he was discharged as Ordinary Seaman, Feb. 14, 1865, expiration of service." *Post Records.*

He was for some time a member of Storer Post, but not at the time of his death.

Libby, George W.—13th N. H.

"Private, Co. C. Residence or assignment, Newcastle. Date of Muster, Sept. 19, 1862, for 3 years. Mustered out June 21, 1865."

Adjutant General's Records, N. H.

Locke, Edwin W.—U. S. Navy.

"Died in New York." *Stone.*

Locke, Fletcher D.—U. S. Navy.

Locke, John H.—5th N. H.

Member Storer Post, G. A. R.

"First Sergeant, Co. B. Residence or assignment, Portsmouth. Date of Mus-

ter, Oct, 23, 1861, for 3 years. Wounded at Fredericksburg. Va., Dec. 13, 1862. Discharged for disability Jan. 5, 1863."
Adjutant General's Records, N. H.

"Birthplace, Barrington, N. H. Struck in six different places by one minnie ball, at Fredericksburg, Va., Dec. 13, 1862: lost parts of both hands. Died June 15, 1889. He was Commander of Storer Post in 1870, and Quartermaster from the second organization of the Post [1878] until his death. A faithful comrade and an honest man."
Post Records.

Locke, Joseph J.—12th Maine.

"Son of Jeremiah and Hannah A. Locke. . . . Killed at Port Hudson, May 25, 1863, aged 19 years, 6 months. He sleeps—where he fell in defence of his country."
Stone.

"Private, Co. K. Born in Barrington, N. H. Resident of Portsmouth, N. H. Date of Muster, Nov. 20, 1861, for 3 years. Killed May 28 [See above], 1863, at Port Hudson, Louisiana."
Adjutant General's Records, Maine.

Locke, William W.—U. S. Navy.

Lombard, Harry—40th Mass.

Enlisted as "Henry Lombard."
Member Storer Post, G. A. R.
"Harry Lombard, died May 31, 1888."
Stone.

"Private Co. F. Residence, Newburyport, Mass. Enlisted Aug. 20, 1862. Date of Muster, Sept. 3, 1862, for 3 years. Wounded at Drury's Bluff, May 16, 1864. Discharged Jan. 10, 1865."
Adjutant General's Records, Mass.

"Born in France, 1836, and was a soldier in the French army. He served with distinction in the Crimea with the French navy, and received a medal of honor for his bravery and devotion. He was also in the Italian campaign, where he did faithful service. Came to this country. Enlisted [Aug. 20, and mustered] Sept. 3, 1862, as Private in Co. F, 40th Regt., Mass. Infantry. . . . While in the advance on Drury's Bluff. . . . on or about May 15 [16], 1864, he was shot, which wound necessitated amputating the right arm at the shoulder joint, and he, with thousands of others, carried the empty sleeve for the past twenty-five years. . . . He was discharged from the U. S. service January 10, 1865. . . . He died May 23 [31], 1888."
Soldiers Memorial, 1889.

Long, Pierse—Rev. War.

"In memory
of
Col. Pierse Long."
Stone.

"Pierse Long (the father of Col. Pierse Long of Revolutionary memory) was born in Limerick, Ireland, about the commencement of the eighteenth century, and served an apprenticeship with one who did business with America; and by him was sent out with goods, the manufacture of Ireland, to this town, in the year 1730." Here he settled, married, and had three children; one son, and two daughters; the latter died unmarried. "Pierse Long, the senior, died in 1740."

"Pierse Long, Jr. (afterwards Col. Long), was born in 1739. He received instruction in the elements of education from the celebrated teacher, Samuel Hale. At the age of fourteen, Pierse was apprenticed as a clerk to Robert Trail [Traill], an emigrant from Scotland, and a distinguished merchant of Portsmouth. At the close of his apprenticeship, Pierse Long was established in business by Mr. Trail [Traill], as a shipping merchant, which he continued to prosecute with success until the war of the Revolution.

In this Mr. Long took an early and decided part, and in 1775 was chosen one of the delegates to the first provincial Congress, convened at Exeter. In this office he continued for some time, acting also about this period as one of the Committee of Safety for Portsmouth, and was engaged with Langdon, Pickering, Drown, and about forty other citizens, in surprising and capturing the fort at the mouth of Portsmouth harbor.

Pierse Long continued to fill different offices under the then province and town until May, 1776, when the provincial Legislature appointed him to the command of the First New Hampshire regiment. . . . This regiment continued in the service of the Province until July 15, 1776, when, it being determined by the general government to receive into the service no more provincial troops, it was disbanded, but immediately rëenlisted into the Continental service, under Pierse Long as Colonel and commander.

This regiment continued to be stationed at the forts around Portsmouth harbor (a company in Portsmouth being stationed near the Old South) until October [November 23], 1776, when it received orders to march to the Canada border, near Lake Champlain [to reinforce the army at Ticonderoga, and marched for that post in February following].

It reached there safely in about twenty days; and reporting for duty to Gen. St. Clair, Col. Long was assigned to the command of Fort Independence, across the Lake, with his own and Col. Carleton's regiments; and at the same time was made Brigadier General, by brevet.

The lake being closed with ice during the latter part of the fall, the winter and part of the spring, nothing of note occurred until about the middle of June, 1777, when the English flotilla of many guns advancing by water, to be joined by Gen. Burgoyne, with ten thousand English, Canadians, Tories, and Indians, by land, it was determined by Gen. St. Clair, in a council of officers, to abandon his position with his small army of three thousand men, and retreat with the American flotilla up through Lake George, towards Fort Edward.

Col. Long was entrusted with the command of the flotilla, consisting of one schooner of sixteen guns, one of ten, and several smaller crafts, with orders to blow up the vessels to prevent their falling into the hands of the enemy,—which was accomplished after they had disembarked his own and Col. Carleton's regiment at Skenesborough.

Leaving Skenesborough, the troops proceeded on towards Saratoga, and the next day (July 6) Col. Long and his command was overtaken by the British ninth regiment, under the command of Col. Hayes. An action ensued, in which the British were beaten, and retreating left the field in the possession of the Americans.

At about this time, the period for which the troops had enlisted having expired, they all asked and received their discharge, officers as well as men, excepting Edward Evans, chaplain; Noah Emery, paymaster; and Lieut. or Col. [Lieutenant] Meshach Bell, and Col. Long's servant, James Mullen.

These, with Col. Long, continued on to Saratoga, and there volunteered their services to the commander-in-chief [General Gates], and assisted in the capture of General Burgoyne and his army [who surrendered October 16, 1777].

Col. Long being ill, arrived in Portsmouth, Dec. 6 [1777]; and continued confined to his house for six months, with the disorder usual to camps; nor did he entirely recover till a year had expired. As soon as he had sufficiently recovered his health he resumed his mercantile pursuits, but at the same time suffered from attacks of the gout, and sometimes could not move without the aid of crutches.

In 1784 he was appointed by the State of New Hampshire a delegate to the old Congress, which post he filled through three or four successive years till 1786 [1784-5-6]. From the year 1786 to 1789 [1788-9—N. H. Manual.] he was elected State Senator or Councillor, and in 1788 was delegate to the Convention to adopt the present Constitution [of the United States], and gave his influence and vote for its reception by New Hampshire.

When Washington was chosen President, he appointed Col. Long Collector of the Customs at Portsmouth: but before he had taken possession of his office, he was found dead in his bed. He retired in apparent health, but died without any previous warning, of (as it was supposed) gout in the stomach, at the early age of fifty, April 3, 1789. His remains are interred in the lot in the Proprietors' burying ground, belonging to his son, at the western end of the granite monuments [monument]. Col. Long was a handsome, portly man, of unblemished christian character, amiable and courteous, a correct merchant and a good soldier."
Rambles About Portsmouth, First Series.

An interesting account of the retreat of the Americans from Fort Ticonderoga in 1777, with special mention of Col. Long's services, will be found in Irving's "Life of Washington," New York, 1882, Vol. III. pages 103-110.

Col. Pierse Long was twice married and had three children. Hon. George Long, a successful shipmaster and merchant of Portsmouth, born July 4, 1762, who died April 8, 1849; the father of Mrs. Henry H. Ladd and the late Samuel P. Long of Portsmouth, and of the late Commodore John Collings Long, U. S. Navy, of Portsmouth and Exeter, N. H., who was a midshipman on the "Constitution" when she captured the British frigate "Java," Dec. 29, 1812. Abigail, who married George W. Prescott, and died at St. Bartholomews, in 1793. Mary, who married Col. Tobias Lear, private secretary to Gen. Washington, April 22, 1790, and died of yellow-fever in the family of Gen. Washington, at Philadelphia, in 1791.

A beautiful Memorial Record Book was presented to Storer Post, G. A. R., on its twenty-fifth anniversary, celebrated November 11, 1892, by Mrs. Henry H. Ladd, of Portsmouth, in memory of her grandfather, Col. Pierse Long. A full account of the presentation was printed in the *Portsmouth Daily Evening Times*, of November 15, 1892, and the following vote was passed at the next meeting of the Post:

"Resolved, That the earnest thanks of Storer Post are hereby tendered to Mrs. Marcy E. Ladd, of Portsmouth, for the magnificent volume recently presented by her to the Post in memory of her grandfather, Colonel Pierse Long of the Revolutionary army; and the Post gladly accepts the opportunity to inscribe therein the record of Colonel Long and the Personal War Sketches of its Comrades, for future preservation."

Lynch, Timothy—U. S. Navy.

Member Storer Post, G. A. R.

"Born in Ireland, 1835, and entered service August 25, 1863, as Ordinary Seaman, U. S. N., for term of 1 year, and was discharged August 25, 1864, his term of enlistment having expired."

Soldiers Memorial, 1887.

Lyon, John H.—U. S. Navy.

Marden, John H.—10th N. H.

"Private, Co. G. Residence or assignment, Portsmouth. Date of Muster, Sept. 4, 1862, for 3 years. Mustered out June 21, 1865."

Adjutant General's Records, N. H.

Marden, John L.—2nd Mass. Cav.

"Killed in a skirmish near Charleston [Charlestown], Va." *Stone.*

"Private, Troop K. Residence, Boston, Ward 6. Enlisted Dec. 8, 1863. Date of Muster, Dec. 8, 1863, for 3 years. Killed in action at Charlestown, Va., Aug. 27, 1864."

Adjutant General's Records, Mass.

Marshall, Christopher J.—2nd N. H.

"A kind Husband and affectionate Father." *Stone.*

"Corporal, Co. K. Residence or assignment, Portsmouth. Date of Muster, June 8, 1861, for 3 years. Wounded and missing at Bull Run, Va., July 21, 1861. Gained from missing. Discharged on account of wounds, July 18, 1862."

Adjutant General's Records, N. H.

Marston, Albert S.—5th N. H.

"Albert Storer Marston."

"No pain, no grief, no anxious fear,
Can reach the peaceful sleeper here."

Stone.

"Private, Co. H. Recruit. Residence or assignment, Portsmouth. Date of Muster, Aug. 11, 1863, for 3 years. Wounded slightly at Sailor's Creek, Va., April 6, 1865. Appointed Corporal, April 8, 1865. Discharged at Philadelphia, Pa., June 6, 1865."

Adjutant General's Records, N. H.

Marston, Joshua B.—35th Mass.

Member Storer Post, G. A. R.

"Enlisted in Co. B, 35th Mass. Vols., Aug. 6th, 1862; wounded at the battle of Antietam, Va. [Md.], Sept. 17th, 1862."

Stone.

"Private, Co. B. Residence, Newburyport, Mass. Enlisted Aug. 6, 1862. Date of Muster, Aug 19, 1862, for 3 years. Discharged for disability Jan. 12, 1863."

Adjutant General's Records, Mass.

"Birthplace, Portsmouth."

Post Records.

Mates, James—U. S. Navy.

Maxwell, Wm. H. H.—5th N. H.

Enlisted as "William H. Maxwell."

"Killed while on a skirmish at Sailor's Creek, Va. . . . God grant that it was not a vain sacrifice." *Stone.*

"Private, Co. K. Recruit. Residence or assignment, Portsmouth. Date of Muster, Aug. 10, 1863, for 3 years. Promoted to Corporal. Killed in action at Sailor's Creek, Va., April 6, 1865."

Adjutant General's Records, N. H.

McClintock, Henry M.—War 1812.

"Henry M. McClintock, U. S. Navy, died at sea, July 24, 1817, aged 19."

Stone.

"Midshipman, 18 June, 1812. Died 28 July, 1817 [See above]."

Hamersly's General Navy Register.

"Died, at sea, of the yellow-fever, on the 28th July last [1817] on board the brig Fanny, Captain Merrill, Mr. Henry McClintock, a Midshipman in the Navy of the United States, being on a furlough, aged 20 years [See above]. On board the various ships he served during the last war he did his duty promptly and with ability, securing the approbation of his officers and the thanks of his country."

Portsmouth Oracle, August 16, 1817.

McClintock, John—Rev. War.

"John McClintock,
Died
Nov. 13, 1855,
Aged 94 yrs."

Stone.

"The late John McClintock.—It becomes our duty this week to record the departure of another of our venerable citizens, in the death, on Tuesday afternoon last [Nov. 13, 1855], of John McClintock, Esq., Naval Officer for the Port of Portsmouth, in the 95th year of his age.

"Capt. John McClintock was the son of the Rev. Dr. Samuel McClintock of Greenland, N. H., who was Chaplain in the army of the Revolution, and was at the battle of Bunker Hill. The patriotic clergyman may be seen represented in the engraving of the battle, in his ministerial bands, near the spot where Gen. Warren lies wounded [See below]."

"John McClint ck, who was born on the 28th of August, 1761, entered the service at the age of about 16, in the private armed ship 'Alexander,' of 20 guns, under Captain Thomas Simpson, who afterwards succeeded Paul Jones in command of the 'Ranger.' At the age of 17, John McClintock was Master's Mate, and was entrusted with conducting a prize into the West Indies. He remained in the service four years, lacking one month—but not being in any public ship he received no pension for revolutionary services."

"After the peace, John McClintock entered the merchant service, and was before the close of the last century shipmaster and owner. He met with losses by the French Spoilations in 1797, of over $10,000, for which his government received a remuneration, but none ever reached him--nor did he ever dispose of a dollar of his claims to any one.

After leaving the ocean he followed mercantile pursuits in this city, and ever manifested a high sense of honor and integrity in his dealings and intercourse—and enjoyed the confidence and esteem of all the leading men of his times. He was of a vigorous constitution, and strengthened it by a temperate and industrious course of life.

Under Harrison's administration he was appointed Naval Officer of this port, and when his term of office expired in August, 1854, President Pierce renewed his commission."

"The world may perhaps be challenged to produce another man who performed the daily duties of a responsible public office, in the full possession of his faculties, until within five years of a century in age.

But he has now gone—and with him departs our last living chronicle of the American Revolution—the last intelligent tie which bound us with those patriots and heroes who achieved the blessings under which our country has acquired her high position among the nations. Yes, the Patriarch of the Revolution, who has so long been left to tell us of the spirit of our fathers—the Man who by his noble spirit, his industrious habits, his upright life and stern integrity, has inspired a veneration for the men of a former age, is now no more—and none can fill his place."

Portsmouth Journal, Nov. 17, 1855.

McClintock, Samuel—Rev. War.

"To the memory of
Samuel McClintock, D. D.,
who died April 27th, 1804,
in the 72d year of his age
& the 48th year of his ministry.
His Body rests here in the
certain hope of a resurrection to life & immortality, when Christ shall appear a second time to destroy the last enemy death & to consummate the great design of his mediatorial Kingdom."

Stone.

"Staff Roll of Col. John Stark's, Col. James Reed's and Col. Enoch Poor's Regiments, from the 23d Day of April, 1775, to the first day of August following—"

"Samuel Macclintock.—Rank, Chap'ain, of Col. Stark's regiment.—Time in service, 1 month.—Amount of wages, £6."

N. H. State Papers, Vol. XIV.

"In the picture [by Trumbull] of the battle of Bunker Hill, representing the fall of Gen. Warren, may be seen in the group a clergyman arrayed in his bands, who appears to be deeply interested in the battle. That man was the Rev. Samuel McClintock, D. D., of Greenland, N. H., the father of the venerable John McClintock, who [served in a private armed ship in the Revolution and] died in Portsmouth a few years since [Nov. 13, 1855] at the age of 94, retaining his mental and physical faculties to the last [See above]."

William McClintock, (the father of Dr. Samuel McClintock) was born in Scotland; early removed to Londonderry, Ireland; and after the siege of that place in 1688 9, came to this country and settled on Mystic river.

"Dr. Samuel McClintock was born in 1732. He was educated at Princeton College," and soon after finishing his studies became minister of the church at Greenland.

"During the Revolution he strongly espoused the side of the people, . . . and was Chaplain at the battle of Bunker Hill."

"Three of his sons perished in the war. One of them, Nathaniel, received a collegiate education at Harvard, but the war breaking out he joined General Washington, and was raised to the rank of Major of Brigade. ["He was with Washington at the memorable capture of the Hessians at Trenton," Dec. 25, 1776.] He was in the New Hampshire line at the battles before the capture of Burgoyne on the 19th of September and the 7th of October [1777]. After the capture, his regiment was ordered South. . . . He was then (although he had not reached 21 years of age) raised to the rank of Major of the line, over all the older Captains. As he was therefore regarded with jealousy by those lower than himself in rank, he resigned his commission and returned home. He was induced to take the command of a company of marines which went out in a ship-of-war, the 'Raleigh,' and soon after perished in an engagement. Another son of Dr. McClintock was an officer at the battle of Trenton and there slain: and a third was lost at sea, serving as a Midshipman, and afterwards as a Lieutenant, in a ship-of-war."

Rev. Mr. McClintock "was loved and esteemed by his parish, and in the latter part of his life received the Diploma of Doctor of Divinity from Princeton College where he was educated."

"History informs us that during the battle of Bunker Hill" Rev. Samuel McClintock "knelt on the field, with hands upraised, and grey head uncovered; and, while the bullets whistled around him, prayed for the success of the compatriots, and the deliverance of his country.

This rare incident prompted the following beautiful ode from the pen of Mrs. Lydia H. Sigourney."

THE PRAYER ON BUNKER HILL.

"It was an hour of fear and dread—
High rose the battle-cry,
And round, in heavy volumes, spread
The war-cloud to the sky.
'Twas not, as when in rival strength
Contending nations meet,
Or love of conquest madly hurls
A monarch from his seat:

Yet one was there, unused to tread
The path of mortal strife,
Who but the Saviour's flock had fed
Beside the fount of life.
He knelt him where the black smoke wreathed—
His head was bowed and bare,—
While, for an infant land he breathed
The agony of prayer.

The column, red with early morn,
May tower o'er Bunker's height,
And proudly tell a race unborn
Their patriot fathers' might:—
But thou, O patriarch, old and grey,
Thou prophet of the free,
Who knelt among the dead that day,
What fame shall rise to thee?

It is not meet that brass or stone
Which feel the touch of time,
Should keep the record of a faith
That woke thy deed sublime;
We trace it to the tablet fair,
Which glows when stars wax pale,
A promise that the good man's prayer
Shall with his God prevail."

Rambles About Portsmouth, Second Series.

McClure, James G.—U. S. M. C.

McDonald, James—U. S. N. & U. S. M. C.

McDuffee, John—U. S. Navy.

McKone, James—U. S. Navy.

"By foreign hands thy dying eyes were closed,
By foreign hands thy decent limbs composed
By foreign hands thy grave adorned
By strangers honored and by strangers mourned."

Stone.

McLeoud, John—U. S. Navy.

McPherson, Alexander—U. S. M. C.

"Born in Paisley, Scotland."

Stone.

Enlisted March 5, 1862, in U. S. M. C., as Private. Promoted to Corporal. Discharged March 5, 1866.

Mead, Cornelius—U. S. Navy.

Mead, Patrick—16th Mass. & V. R. C.

"Private, Co. D. Residence, Lowell, Mass. Enlisted July 12, 1861. Date of Muster, July 12, 1861, for 3 years. Wounded May 3, 1863. Transferred to the Veteran Reserve Corps. Discharged July 20, 1864."

Adjutant General's Records, Mass.

Melmoth, Hector—U. S. M. C.

Merrill, George A.—U. S. Navy.

Mills, William J.—16th N. H.

Member Storer Post, G. A. R.

"Private, Co. K. Residence, Portsmouth. Date of Muster, Nov. 15, 1862, for 9 months. Mustered out Aug. 20, 1863."

Adjutant General's Records, N. H.

"Birthplace, Gorham, Maine."

Post Records.

Mitchell, James—16th N. H.

"Private, Co. K. Residence or assignment, Portsmouth. Date of Muster, Oct. 25, 1862, for 9 months. Died of disease near Vicksburg, Miss., Aug. 9, 1863."

Adjutant General's Records, N. H.

Moore, Andrew J.—35th Mass.

"Co. K, 35th Regt. Mass. Vol. Killed in the Battle of Antietam, Sept. 17, 1862. . . . Son of Fred W. and Clementina Moore."

Stone.

"Private, Co. K. Residence, Roxbury, Mass. Enlisted Aug. 1, 1862. Date of

Muster, Aug. 10, 1862, for 3 years. Not heard from since the battle of Antietam [See above]."

Adjutant General's Records, Mass.

Moore, John—13th N. H.

Member Stoier Post, G. A. R.

"That dear arm on which I rested,
Is no longer at my side,
And the voice I loved to follow,
Never more will be my guide."

Stone.

"Private, Co. K. Residence or assignment, Portsmouth. Date of Muster, Sept. 20, 1862, for 3 years. Promoted to Corporal, May 17, 1865. Mustered out June 21, 1865."

Adjutant General's Records, N. H.

"Birthplace, New Hampshire"

Post Records.

Moore, John H.—10th N. H.

"Co. G, 10th N. H. Regt. Killed in a Skirmish before Petersburg, July 2, 1864 [See below]. . . . Son of Fred W. and Clementina Moore." *Stone.*

"Private, Co. G. Residence, Portsmouth. Date of Muster, Sept. 4, 1862, for 3 years. Wounded June 23, 1864. Died of wounds, July 2, 1864."

Adjutant General's Records, N. H.

Moore, Thomas R.—U. S. Navy.

Moore, William—Mass. Vols.

Morrill, John H.—16th N. H.

"Sergeant, Co. K. Residence or assignment, Portsmouth. Date of Muster, Oct. 25, 1862, for 9 months. Promoted to First Sergeant May 16, 1863. Mustered out Aug. 20, 1863."

Adjutant General's Records, N. H.

Morrison, John H.—10th N. H.

"Son of John and Catherine Morrison. . . . Died in the Washington Hospital. . . . May he rest in peace. Erected by his numerous friends in Portsmouth." *Stone.*

"Private, Co. G. Residence, Portsmouth. Date of Muster, Sept. 4, 1862, for 3 years. Died of disease at Washington, D. C., Nov. 3, 1862."

Adjutant General's Records, N. H.

Morse, Edgar L.—4th Mass.

"Private, Co. K. Residence, Taunton, Mass. Enlisted ——. Date of Muster, Sept 23, 1862, for 9 months. Discharged Aug. 28 1863, expiration of service."

Adjutant General's Records, Mass.

Moses, Edward—U. S. Navy.

"Acting Master, 17 May, 1862. Died 18 May, 1864."

Hamersly's General Navy Register.

"Died at Portsmouth, N. H., May 18, 1864." *Navy Register, 1865.*

Moses, Levi Jr.—U. S. Navy.

"Drowned from U. S. Steamer 'Flag,' off Cape Hatteras." *Stone.*

Moulton, Charles W.—3rd N. H.

His stone reads incorrectly—"Chas. Moulton, U. S. Navy."

"Private, Co. K. Residence, Portsmouth. Date of Muster, Aug. 24, 1861, for 3 years. Reënlisted Feb 11, 1864. Private, Co. K. Residence or assignment, Portsmouth. Date of Muster, Feb. 11, 1864, for 3 years. Promoted to Corporal, March 1, 1865. Promoted to Sergeant, May 1, 1865. Mustered out July 20, 1865."

Adjutant General's Records, N. H.

Moulton, David A.—U. S. N. & 2nd Mass. Cav.

Enlisted as "David Moulton."

"Seaman, U. S. Navy. Born in Great Falls, N. H. Residence or assignment, Boston. Enlisted Sept. 14, 1861, for 2 years. Served on U. S. vessels 'Brandywine,' 'Morse' and 'Sabine.' Discharged from U. S. S. 'Sabine,' Sept. 18, 1863, expiration of enlistment.

Private, Troop A, 2nd Mass. Cavalry. Residence, Portsmouth, N. H. Assignment, Boxford, Mass. Enlisted April 11, 1864. Date of Muster, April 11, 1864, for 3 years. Mustered out July 20, 1865."

Adjutant General's Records, Mass.

Moulton, Thomas—Mex. War.

Murray, John—Mex. War & 5th N. H.

"Capt.
John Murray,
born in the City of New York, 1825,
Served in the Mexican War in 1847,
on recommendation of Lieut. Col. Belton,
received a certificate of merit from
President Fillmore,
Commissioned Captain of Co. D, 5th N. H.
Volunteers, Oct. 12, 1861,
He fell early in the battle of
Fredericksburg,
Dec. 13, 1862, while leading a gallant band
of the Defenders of his Country.
A kind Father and Husband, a patriotic
Citizen, a brave and faithful Soldier and
Officer. His last words were—

'That Flag never was and never shall be disgraced!'
Erected by his Portsmouth friends."
Stone.

"Captain, Co. D., 5th N. H. Residence, Newcastle. Commissioned Oct. 12, 1861. Killed at Fredericksburg, Va., Dec. 13, 1862."
Adjutant General's Records, N. H.

"Capt. John Murray of Company D, 5th N. H. Volunteers, was killed at the battle of Fredericksburg, Dec. 13, 1862.

It was stated by Col. Cross, who commanded the famous 'Fighting Fifth,' that Capt. Murray left the hospital against the express orders of the surgeon on the morning of the day of the battle, saying his men should never go into a fight without him while he lived.

In the disastrous charge upon the stone wall, after three color bearers of Company D had been shot down in succession, the colors were taken by Capt. Murray, and he was pressing on at the head of the remnant of his company when he fell, shot through the head, his body being nearer the stone wall than that of any other Union soldier. Two days after his death his commission as Major arrived at regimental headquarters.

Capt. Murray is said . . . to have been the first man from Newcastle killed in the war. His body was brought home, and on Sunday, the 21st of December, a bitter cold day, his funeral services were held in the Congregational church, Rev. Lucius Alden officiating, and the church being crowded with the citizens, including all the town officials.

He was buried under arms by a company of State militia composed wholly of Newcastle men.

Capt. Murray served in the regular army during the Mexican war as a member of Company K, 3rd U. S. Artillery, and on the recommendation of Lieut Col. Francis S. Belton, who commanded that regiment, was granted a certificate of merit for special gallantry at the battle of Chapultepec, near the City of Mexico, Sept. 13, 1847, and this certificate, signed by Millard Fillmore as President of the United States, and Charles M. Conrad as Secretary of War, is still preserved."
Boston Daily Globe, May 30, 1892.

Nash, Joseph E.—16th N. H.

Member Storer Post, G. A. R.
"Private, Co. K. Residence, Portsmouth. Date of Muster, Oct. 25, 1862, for 9 months. Mustered out Aug. 20, 1863."
Adjutant General's Records, N. H.

"Birthplace, Boston, Mass."
Post Records.

Neal, Franklin W.—16th N. H.

"Private, Co. K. Residence or assignment, Portsmouth. Date of Muster, Oct. 25, 1862, for 9 months. Discharged to date Aug. 20, 1863."
Adjutant General's Records, N. H.

Nellings, William—U. S. M. C.

Newkirk, Peter—20th Mass.

"Killed in battle at Hatches [Hatcher's] Run, Va., Oct. 27, 1864." *Stone.*

"Private, Co. A. Residence, Boston. Enlisted Aug. 26, 1862. Date of Muster, Aug. 26, 1862, for 3 years. Reënlisted Dec. 20, 1863. Promoted to Sergeant. Killed in action at Hatcher's Run, Va., Oct. 29 [See above], 1864."
Adjutant General's Records, Mass.

Norton, James—19th Mass.

"A native of Ballygar, Co. Galway, Ireland."
Stone.

"Private, Co. E. Residence, Boston. Enlisted July 25, 1861. Date of Muster, July 26, 1861, for 3 years. Discharged for disability Jan. 29, 1862."
Adjutant General's Records, Mass.

Norton, James—19th Mass.

Nowell, Andrew C.—8th N. H.

"Andrew Craigie, son of Henry and Abigail Nowell. . . . Died in Hospital, near New Orleans, La." *Stone.*

"Private, Co. D. Residence or assignment, Raymond. Date of Muster, Dec. 20, 1861, for 3 years. Died of disease at Camp Parapet, La., Aug 16, 1862."
Adjutant General's Records, N. H.

Noyes, Leverett W.—U. S. Navy.

Enlisted as "Joseph Noyes."
"Joseph Noyes, U. S. Navy." *Stone.*

Nutter, William H.—13th N. H.

Enlisted as "Henry Nutter."
"Private, Co. E. Residence or assignment, Portsmouth. Date of Muster, Sept. 23, 1862, for 3 years. Wounded at Fredericksburg, Va., Dec. 13, 1862. Discharged for disability at Washington, D. C., Feb. 5, 1864."
Adjutant General's Records, N. H.

Olney, Jesse—3rd U. S. Art.

Oxford, William F.—2nd N. H.

"Wounded at the battle of Bull Run. Died at Richmond." *Stone.*

"Private, Co. K. Residence, Portsmouth. Date of Muster, June 8, 1861, for 3 years. Captured at Bull Run, Va., July 21, 1861. Died at Richmond, Va., Aug. 5, 1861."

Adjutant General's Records, N. H.

Son of John R. Oxford. He was the first of many sons of Portsmouth, who lost their lives in the War of the Rebellion.

Palmer, Nathaniel F.—2nd N. H.

"Nathaniel F.,
Son of Nathaniel M.
& Eunice Palmer.
died at Harrison's Landing, Va.,
Aug 9, 1862,
Aged 19 yrs.
A member of Co. K, 2d Regt. N. H. V.
Here lies a patriot soldier, who
died in his country's cause.
He now is resting in a brighter
and better land.
Kind friends bore him to his
silent resting-place.
Erected by the Fire Department of
Portsmouth, of which he was a member."
Stone.

"Private, Co. K. Residence or assignment, Portsmouth. Date of Muster, June 8, 1861, for 3 years. Died of disease at Harrison's Landing, Va., Aug. 9, 1862."

Adjutant General's Records, N. H.

"Nathaniel F. Palmer, a native of Portsmouth, and member of Company K, 2nd Regiment, N. H. Volunteers, died Aug. 9, 1862, near Harrison's Landing, Va., at the age of 19 years. The body was removed to Harrison's Landing, where it was embalmed and forwarded by Company K, at their own expense, to his family in this city [Portsmouth].

Mr. Palmer was the first man who was enlisted by Capt. William O. Sides (the latter having been himself the first man in New Hampshire to enlist), and was the first man who died and was brought home after the regiment was mustered into the service of the United States.

The funeral services were held in the State Street Methodist Episcopal church on Sunday afternoon, Aug. 17, 1862. Rev. R. W. Humphries, pastor of the church, made the address.

The funeral procession was long and imposing. The coffin was appropriately draped with the American flag, and was borne on the shoulders of six of his brother firemen through the streets to Harmony Grove cemetery, where prayer was again offered, and three volleys were fired by the Goodwin Guards over the grave.

The flags throughout the city were displayed at half mast during the day."

Boston Daily Globe, May 30, 1892.

Parker, William A.—U. S Navy.

William Albert Parker.

"Midshipman, 3 July, 1832. Passed Midshipman, 23 June, 1838. Lieutenant, 16 May, 1843. Commander, 28 June, 1861. Retired list, 23 December, 1865. Captain on Retired list, 4 April, 1867."

Hamersly's General Navy Register.

"Died at East Boston, Mass., October 24, 1882." *Navy Register, 1883.*

"Born at Portsmouth, N. H., January 12, 1816. Entered the navy as a Midshipman, July 3, 1832; first service in the U. S. sloop-of-war 'Vincennes,' under the command of Commodore Alexander S. Wadsworth and Capt. John H. Aulick, on the Pacific Station; second cruise was made in the U. S. razee 'Independence,' under the command of Commodore John B. Nicholson, on the coast of Brazil and the Coast of England and Russia, and bearing the Hon. George M. Dallas as Minister to the latter country.

Promoted to the grade of Passed Midshipman on June 23, 1838; thence served in the U. S. line-of-battle-ship 'Ohio,' under command of Commodore Isaac Hull and Capts. Joseph Smith and Lavalette, in the years 1838-41, in the Mediterranean Squadron; the next service was at the rendezvous at Boston, Mass.; in the year 1842, served on board the frigate 'United States,' under commands of Commodore T. Ap Catesby Jones and Capt. James Armstrong, on the Pacific Station.

Promoted to Lieutenant, May 16, 1843, and transferred to the 'Cyane,' Commander C. K. Stribling; the squadron was actively employed, and visited the coast of California and the Sandwich Islands, Chili, Peru, etc.; in 1846, ordered to the U. S. steamer 'Mississippi,' Capt. Andrew Fitzhugh, on the Mexican coast; afterwards under command of Commodore Matthew C. Perry; served in this steamer, and the 'Raritan,' Commodore David Connor, during the Mexican war, till near its termination; in 1848 was attached to the National Observatory at Washington, then under the superintendence of Lieut. Matthew F. Maury; the next service was in the 'Raritan,' Commodore Foxhall A. Parker and Capt. Benjamin Page; was present at the seige and capture of Vera Cruz, Tabasco, and other places; in 1851, served on board the receiving-ship 'Franklin;' in 1852, was ordered to the sloop 'Portsmouth,' T. A. Dornin, commander, on the Pacific Station, and returned home in 1855; in 1856, was stationed at the rendezvous, Boston, for about two years; in 1859-60, commanded the store-ship 'Release,' and was ordered to the Mediterranean Squadron at Spezia; from thence to the squadron under Commodore Shubrick, to Paraguay, for the settlement of difficulties with that country, and thence to the African Squadron; after that cruise, served as first lieutenant at the Boston Navy Yard, under command of Capt. William L. Hudson and Commander Henry K. Thatcher; on the breaking out of the Rebellion was ordered to command the steamer 'Cambridge,' and served on the North Atlantic Blockade, off the coasts of Virginia and North Carolina, under the command of Commodores L. M. Goldsborough, Samuel Phillips Lee, and David D. Porter, and under the latter commanded the Fifth Division of the North Blockade, which included more than 20 vessels of different kinds and several monitors; detached from that duty in the early part of 1865, having served continuously from the beginning of the war.

Promoted to Commander, June 28, 1861; placed on the retired list, December 23, 1865; from 1866-69, commanded the receiving ship 'Independence,' on the California Station.

Promoted to Captain, on the retired list, April 19, 1869 [See above]; last duty was as inspector of lighthouses, seventh district, which included the whole coast of the Gulf of Mexico, from Cedar Keys, Fla., to the southern border of the State of Texas. Total sea service, 22 years; shore or other duty, 12 years and 9 months."

Hamersly's Naval Encyclopedia.

Parks, Edward H.—U. S. Navy.

Sometimes called "David Parks."

Parks, J. S.—U. S. Navy.

Parks, Thomas B.—13th N. H.

"Son of Elisha and Drewsilla Parks."

Stone.

"Private, Co. K. Residence or assignment, Portsmouth. Date of Muster, Sept. 20, 1862, for 3 years. Discharged for disability at Washington, D. C., Feb. 23, 1863."

Adjutant General's Records, N. H.

Parrott, Enoch G.—U. S. Navy.

"In memory of
Enoch Greenleafe Parrott,
Rear Admiral, U. S. Navy,
who died May 10, 1879, Aged 63 years.
Generous. Truthful. Just.
A brave and loyal officer.
Africa, 1832.
Mexico, 1848.
Port Royal, 1861.
Fort Fisher, 1865.
Charleston, 1865.
Asiatic Squadron, 1873.

Monument.

"General Order.

Navy Department,
Washington, June 4, 1879.

The Secretary of the Navy, with deep regret, announces to the service the death, at New York, on the 10th of May last, of Rear Admiral Enoch G. Parrott.

Rear Admiral Parrott received his first appointment December 10, 1831, and during his long service was faithful and zealous in the discharge of his duties. During the rebellion he was actively engaged, and participated in the battles of Port Royal, South Carolina, and Fort Fisher, North Carolina. He commanded the Mare Island Navy Yard in 1871 and 1872, and the naval force; on the Asiatic station in 1873, which last command his failing health compelled him to relinquish.

On the day after the receipt of this order, the flags of the Navy Yards and Naval Stations, and of all ships in commission, will be displayed at half-mast from sunrise to sunset, and thirteen minute guns will be fired at noon from each Navy Yard and Station, flag-ship and vessel acting singly.

R. W. Thompson,
Secretary of the Navy."

"Midshipman, 10 December, 1831. Passed Midshipman, 15 June, 1837. Lieutenant, 8 September, 1841. Commander, 24 April, 1861. Captain, 25 July, 1866. Commodore, 22 April, 1870. Rear-Admiral, 8 November, 1873. Retired list, 4 April, 1874. Died 10 May, 1879."

Hamersly's General Navy Register.

"Died in New York, May 10, 1879."

Navy Register, 1880.

"Born in New Hampshire. Appointed from New Hampshire, December 10, 1831; attached to schooner 'Boxer,' Brazil Squadron, 1832-4; attached to sloop 'Natchez,' Brazil Squadron, 1835; Navy Yard, Boston, 1837. Promoted to Passed Midshipman, June 15, 1837; brig 'Consort,' on surveying duty, 1840.

Commissioned as Lieutenant, September 8, 1841; was engaged in the operations under Commodore Perry against Beraly, and the neighboring towns on the west coast of Africa, December, 1843; and was with all the landing parties.

sloop 'Saratoga,' coast of Africa, 1843; frigate 'Congress,' Pacific Squadron, 1846-8. During the war with Mexico, while serving in the 'Congress,' was with Fremont's Expedition from Monterey to Los Angelos, at which place there was a slight engagement; was at the capture of Guaymas and Mazatlan, and in two skirmishes at the last-named place. The 'Congress' received the thanks of the President and the Department. Receiving-ship 'Boston,' 1850; sloop 'St. Louis,' Mediterranean Squadron, 1852-3; sloop 'St. Mary's,' Pacific Squadron, 1854-5; Naval Observatory, Washington, 1857-8; special duty, 1859.

Commissioned as Commander, April, 1861; was with the expedition which destroyed Norfolk Navy Yard, April, 1861; in the brig 'Perry' at the time of the capture of the rebel privateer 'Savannah,' which resisted; received for this the commendation of the Department; commanding steamer 'Augusta,' 1861-3; in the 'Augusta' participated in the battle of Port Royal, under Rear Admiral DuPont, and subsequently engaged the rebel rams at the time of their sortie from Charleston, January 13 [31], 1863, and was on this occasion under the fire of the rebel batteries in Charleston harbor; commanding iron-clad 'Canonicus,' N. A. B. Squadron, 1864-5; in the 'Canonicus,' participated in the engagement with Howlett's Battery and the iron clads on James River, June 21, 1864; and in the subsequent engagement with Howlett's Battery; commanding iron-clad 'Monadnock,' in the attacks under Rear Admiral Porter on Fort Fisher, in December 1864, and January 1865; and subsequently, under Rear Admiral Dahlgren, was present at the surrender of Charleston; commanding receiving ship, 'Boston,' 1865-8.

Commissioned as Captain, July 25, 1866; Navy Yard [Waiting orders], Portsmouth, New Hampshire, 1869. Commissioned as Commodore, 1870 [Commandant Navy Yard, Boston, 1871]; Commandant Navy Yard, Mare Island, 1871-2; Asiatic Station, 1872-3. Commissioned as Rear Admiral, November 8, 1873. Died in 1879."

Hamersly's Naval Records, 1890.

"Upon recommendation of the President.

A resolution tendering the thanks of Congress to Captain Samuel F. DuPont, and officers, petty officers, seamen, and marines under his command, for the victory at Port Royal.

That the thanks of Congress be, and they are hereby, tendered to Captain Samuel F. DuPont, and through him to the officers, petty officers, seamen, and marines attached to the squadron under his command, for the decisive and splendid victory achieved at Port Royal on the 7th day of November, last.

Approved February 22, 1862."

Hamersly's General Navy Register.

"A resolution tendering the thanks of Congress to Rear-Admiral David D. Porter, and to the officers, petty officers, seamen, and marines under his command, for their gallantry and good conduct in the recent capture of Fort Fisher.

That the thanks of Congress are hereby presented to Rear-Admiral David D. Porter, and to the officers, petty officers, seamen, and marines under his command, for the unsurpassed gallantry and skill exhibited by them in the attacks upon Fort Fisher and the brilliant and decisive victory by which that important work has been captured from the rebel forces and placed in the possession and under the authority of the United States, and for their long and faithful services and unwavering devotion to the cause of the country in the midst of the greatest difficulties and dangers.

Sec. 2. And be it further resolved, That the President of the United States be requested to communicate this resolution to Admiral Porter, and through him to the officers, seamen, and marines under his command.

Approved January 24, 1865."

Hamersly's General Navy Register.

"Admiral Parrott was born in Portsmouth, N. H. [Nov. 27, 1815.] . . . His father [Enoch Greenleafe Parrott, senior] was a prominent merchant of Portsmouth, and his uncle, John F. Parrott, was for several years [1819-1825] United States Senator from New Hampshire. Robert P. Parrott, the inventor of the celebrated gun that bears his name, was the cousin of the Admiral."

New York Herald, May 11, 1879.

Partridge, George F.—U. S. Navy.

Patch, Charles W.—2nd N. H.

"Charles W. Patch,
Lieut. of Co. K.
2nd Regt. N. H. V.
Died at Gettysburgh, Pa.,
July 10, 1863, from wounds
received in Battle of July 2nd.
Aged 33 years.
God grant that it may not
be a vain sacrifice."

Stone.

"Sergeant, Co. K. Residence or assignment, Portsmouth. Date of Muster, June 8, 1861, for 3 years. Promoted to 1st Sergeant. Promoted to 2d Lieutenant, Co. K. Date of Commission, Aug. 1, 1862. Wounded at Gettysburg, Pa., July 2, 1863. Died of wounds at Gettysburg, Pa., July 10, 1863."

Adjutant General's Records, N. H.

Paul, Joseph W.—1st N. H. H. Art.

"Private, Co. A. Residence or assignment, Portsmouth. Date of Muster, July 18, 1863, for 3 years. Promoted to Corporal, Nov. 1, 1864. Mustered out Sept. 11, 1865."

Adjutant General's Records, N. H.

Payne, Albert L.—16th N. H.

"Private, Co. K. Residence, Portsmouth. Date of Muster, Oct. 25, 1862, for 9 months. Mustered out Aug 20, 1863."

Adjutant General's Records, N. H.

Pearson, George F.—U. S. Navy.

George Frederick Pearson.

"George F. Pearson,
Rear Admiral, U. S. Navy.
Died July 1, 1867.
Not lost but gone before."

Stone.

"Midshipman, 11 March, 1815. Lieutenant, 13 January, 1825. Commander, 8 September, 1841. Captain, 14 September. 1855. Retired list, 21 December, 1861. Commodore on Retired list, 16 July, 1862. Rear Admiral on Retired list. 25 July, 1866. Died 30 June [See above]. 1867."

Hamersly's General Navy Register.

"Died at Portsmouth, N. H., June 30 [See above,] 1867."

Navy Register 1868.

"Pearson, George Frederick, naval officer, born in New Hampshire, 6 Feb., 1796; died in Portsmouth, N. H., 30 June [See above], 1867. He was appointed Midshipman, 11 March, 1815, and cruised in the frigates 'United States' and 'Indedendence' in the Mediterranean in 1816-20, and in the West Indies in 1822-3. He was commissioned Lieutenant, 13 Jan., 1825, commanded the schooner 'Shark' at Norfolk, in 1839, and served at the Portsmouth Navy Yard in 1839-41. He was promoted to Commander on 8 Sept. of the latter year, was in the 'Falmouth' at Norfolk in 1852-3, and became Captain, 14 Sept., 1855. He commanded the steamer 'Powhatan' in the East Indies in 1858-60. During the civil war he rendered valuable service as Commandant of the Portsmouth Navy Yard, which post he held at his death [Commandant Navy Yard, Portsmouth, N. H., 1860-4; commanding Pacific Squadron, 1865-6; waiting orders, 1867]. He was retired by law, being over sixty-two years old, 21 Dec., 1861, and became Commodore on the Retired list, 16 July, 1862, and Rear Admiral, 25 July, 1866."

Appleton's Cyclopædia of American Biography.

He was in command of the U. S. steam frigate "Powhatan," carrying the flag of Commodore Josiah Tatnall (afterwards a flag officer in the Confederate Navy), during her cruise in the East Indies, in the years 1857-60.

An interesting account of this cruise will be found in "China and Japan," by Lieut. James D. Johnston, U. S. N., Executive-Officer of the "Powhatan," Philadelphia, 1861, with full particulars of the affair at the Peiho forts, when Flag Officer Tatnall, declaring that "blood is thicker than water," set aside for a moment the duties of a neutral, and gave help to the English, repulsed by the Chinese—aid which no English Naval officer will ever forget.

Pearson, John H.—16th N. H.

"Son of Stephen B. and Catherine L. Pearson, died Aug. 22, 1863."

"From the tree where hope's bright buds wave,
Pluck flowers for the soldier's hallowed grave."

Stone.

"Private, Co. K. Residence, Portsmouth Date of of Muster, Oct 25, 1862, for 9 months. Mustered out Aug. 20, 1863."

Adjutant General's Records, N. H.

Pender, William P.—10th N. H.

Enlisted as "William Allen."

"William Paton Pender. . . . Killed at Fort Darling, Va." *Stone.*

"Private, Co. A. Recruit. Assignment, Dover [Residence, Portsmouth.]. Date of Muster, Aug. 11, 1863, for 3 years. Killed at Drury's Bluff, Va., May 16, 1864."

Adjutant General's Records, N. H.

Pendexter, Edward—U. S. Navy.

"Acting Ensign, 4 December, 1862. Honorably discharged 31 October, 1865."

Hamersly's General Navy Register.

Perkins, George—War 1812.

"Lost in the Privateer 'Portsmouth,' in the winter of 1815." *Stone.*

"The Privateer 'Portsmouth,' of Portsmouth, was a conspicuous cruising vessel. She was commanded by John Sinclair and made a great many valuable prizes."

Rambles About Portsmouth, Second Series.

Perry, George N.—U. S. Navy.

Peterson, Adrian A.—U. S. Navy.

"Died in Chelsea, Mass., July 27, 1871."
Stone.

"Gunner, 25 October, 1836. Retired list, 21 December, 1861."
Hamersly's General Navy Register.

His death is not entered in the Annual Navy Register.

Pettigrew, William—Mex. War.

Pettigrew, William—U. S. Navy.

Philbrick, Oliver B.—13th N. H.

Enlisted as "Oliver B. Philbrook."

"Private, Co. K. Residence or assignment, Rye. Date of Muster, Sept. 20, 1862, for 3 years. Discharged for disability at Portsmouth, Va., Oct. 7, 1863."
Adjutant General's Records, N. H.

Pickering, Charles W.—U. S. Navy.

"Charles Whipple Pickering,
Commodore, U. S. Navy.
Dec. 23, 1815—Feb. 29, 1888."
Stone.

"Midshipman, 1 May, 1822. Passed Midshipman, 10 June, 1833. Lieutenant, 8 December, 1838. Commander, 14 September, 1855. Captain, 16 July, 1862. Retired List, 1 February, 1867. Commodore on Retired list, 8 December, 1867."
Hamersly's General Navy Register.

"Died at St. Augustine, Florida, February 29, 1888." *Navy Register, 1889.*

"Born in New Hampshire, from which State he was appointed Midshipman, May 22 [1], 1822. In 1822-3 made his first cruise with his uncle, Captain R. T. Spencer [Robert Traill Spence], on board the sloop-of-war 'Cyane', a prize to the 'Constitution', under Commodore Stewart. During this cruise the 'Cyane' was stationed on the coast of Africa, and lost by fever fifty of her officers and crew. On leave, 1824-6; Naval School, New York, 1827; in 1828, attached to sloop-of-war 'Erie', Captain Daniel Turner, West India station; on the return of the 'Erie' to New York, was ordered to the Naval School, but by permission of the Department, was placed at a boarding-school in New York City, where he remained until the summer of 1831; from the summer of 1831 to February, 1834, was attached to the sloop-of-war 'Falmouth,' Captain F. H. Gregory, Pacific Squadron.

Promoted to Passed Midshipman, June 1833; serving at Navy Yard, Boston, during the years 1835-6; from 1837-9, attached to United States frigate 'Fulton', stationed on the United States coast.

Commissioned as Lieutenant, December 8, 1838; from 1840-2, attached to sloop 'Yorktown', Pacific Squadron; from 1844-5 Executive-Officer of the sloop 'Preble', West India and African Squadrons; attached to Navy Yard Portsmouth, New Hampshire, 1846-7; in 1848-9, attached to sloop-of-war 'St. Mary's', Pacific Squadron; commanding the sloop-of-war 'Warren', Pacific Squadron, during the years 1850-1; in 1854, served as Executive-Officer of the sloop 'Cyane', which vessel took out the Darien Expedition, under Lieutenant Strain, who lost seven of his men by starvation. Lieutenant Pickering in his search for that party, was within four hours' march of the head-waters of the Chaquenaque, the course of which it was his intention to follow, when he was apprised by Indian runners of the arrival of Lieutenant Strain and party at Chapagana, Pacific side. Lieutenant Pickering's observations during two successive expeditions from the ship, in search of Strain, convinced him of the utter folly of any attempt to cut a canal at Darien.

After landing Lieutenant Strain with the remainder of his party at New York, the 'Cyane' was ordered to Greytown, Nicaragua, which town, in pursuance of redress, was reduced to ashes, after a bombardment of four hours. Only one house was left standing. In 1855-7, attached to United States Navy Yard, Portsmouth, New Hampshire.

Promoted to Commander, September 14, 1855; in 1859-61, Inspector of the Seventh Light-House District, headquarters at Key West.

Commissioned as Captain, July 15 [16], 1862; in 1862-3, commanding United States steam-sloop 'Kearsarge,' Mediterranean and Western Islands; in 1863-4, commanding United States steam-sloop 'Housatonic,' which was blown up, off Charleston, on the night of February 17, 1864, by a submarine torpedo. As soon as recovered from wounds received on board the 'Housatonic,' took command of the United States steamer 'Vanderbilt,' which vessel participated in the capture of Fort Fisher. Detached from 'Vanderbilt' in August, 1865, and ordered to Portsmouth Navy Yard; detached from Portsmouth Navy Yard, February, 1867, when Captain Pickering went upon the retired list at his own request.

Commissioned as Commodore [from December 8, 1867] in 1871."
Hamersly's Naval Records, 1878.

Pickering, Simeon S.—U. S. Navy.

Place, Charles S.—U. S. Navy.

Place, Leonard—U. S. Navy.

Plaisted, B. Frank P.—U. S. Navy.

"Died at St. Albans, Vt." *Stone.*

Plaisted, Charles E.—2nd N. H.

"Private, Co. K. Residence or assignment, Stratham. Date of Muster, June 8, 1861, for 3 years. Promoted to Corporal, July, 1863. Reënlisted. Corporal, Co. K. Residence or assignment, Portsmouth. Date of Muster, Jan. 1, 1864, for 3 years. Promoted to Sergeant, July, 1864. Promoted to First Sergeant, Sept., 1864. Promoted to Adjutant. Date of Commission, Nov. 1, 1864 Promoted to Captain, Co. B. Date of Commission, Nov. 1, 1865. Not mustered. Mustered out as First Lieutenant and Adjutant, Dec. 19, 1865."

Adjutant General's Records, N. H.

Plaisted, William A.—36th Mass.

"Private, Co. C. Residence, Worcester, Mass. Enlisted Aug. 14, 1862. Date of Muster, Aug 14, 1862, for 3 years. Mustered out June 8, 1865."

Adjutant General's Records, Mass.

Poole, John—20th Maine.

Enlisted as "John Poole, Jr."

"John Poole, Corporal." *Stone.*

"Private, Co. F. Born in Edgecomb, Maine. Resident of Bristol, Maine. Date of Muster, August 29, 1862, for 3 years. Mustered out and honorably discharged —by reason of G. O. No. 77, War Dept., April 28, 1865."

Adjutant General's Records, Maine.

Pottle, Samuel A.—U. S. Navy.

Samuel Augustus Pottle.

"S. C. Pottle, U. S. Navy." *Stone.*

Quint, William Goodwin—2nd N. H.

Enlisted as "William H. Goodwin."

"Private, Co. K. Residence, Lisbon, N. H. Date of Muster, June 8, 1861, for 3 years. Wounded and missing at Bull Run, Va, Aug. 29, 1862. Gained from missing. Discharged for wounds at Philadelphia, Pa., May 21, 1863."

Adjutant General's Records, N. H.

"William Goodwin [of Newington, N. H.], who was a member of the 2nd N. H. Regiment, was severely wounded in battle, and lost the use of one leg: he was drowned along in the sixties, after the war [June 19, 1864], at Portsmouth bridge."

Portsmouth Daily Eve. Times, June 3, 1892.

Ramsdell, John H.—3rd U. S. Art.

Ramsdell, S.—3rd U. S. Art.

Rand, Ammi C.—17th & 2nd N. H.

"Co. K, 2nd N. H. Inf." *Stone.*
See below.

"Private, Co. B, 17th N. H. Residence or assignment, Portsmouth. Date of Muster, Nov. 13, 1862, for 9 months. Consolidated with Co. A, 2nd N. H. V., April 16, 1863.

Private, Co. A, 2nd N. H. Recruit. Transferred from 17th N. H. V., April 16, 1863. Mustered out Oct. 9, 1863."

Adjutant General's Records, N. H.

Rand, Francis W.—9th N. H.

"Died at Camp Nelson, Ky." *Stone.*

"Private, Co. E. Residence or assignment, Rye. Date of Muster, May 15, 1862, for 3 years. Died of disease at Camp Nelson, Ky., Jan. 20, 1864."

Adjutant General's Records, N. H.

Rand, Irving—6th N. H.

Enlisted as "Irving W. Rand."

Buried on farm of Alonzo and Sullivan Rand, Lafayette road, Portsmouth, near the Rye line.

"Private, Co. H. Residence, Rye. Date of Muster, Nov. 28, 1861, for 3 years. Reënlisted Dec. 31, 1863. Corporal, Co. H. Residence or assignment, Portsmouth. Date of Muster, Dec. 31, 1863, for 3 years. Promoted to Sergeant. Wounded at the Mine, July 30, 1864. Died of wounds near Petersburg, Va., Aug. 2, 1864."

Adjutant General's Records, N. H.

Rand, Robert—13th N. H.

"Private, Co. K. Residence or assignment, Portsmouth. Date of Muster, Sept. 20, 1862, for 3 years. Discharged for disability at Fortress Monroe, Va., May 24, 1863."

Adjutant General's Records, N. H.

Randall, Charles W.—U. S. N. & 13th N. H.

Enlisted as "Charles Randall."

Member Storer Post, G. A. R.

"Died Aug. 22, 1887." *Stone.*

"Private, Co. K, 13th N. H. Residence or assignment, Portsmouth. Date of Muster, Sept. 20, 1862, for 3 years. Wounded at Chapin's Farm, Va., Sept. 30, 1864 Mustered out May 27, 1865."

Adjutant General's Records, N. H.

"Born in Portsmouth, N. H., in the year 1837,—Died August 24 [See above], 1887, at the age of fifty years.

Our deceased comrade first entered the U. S. service in 1859, at which time he shipped on board the U. S. S. 'St. Louis,' which was [in 1861] ordered to Florida, to guard Fort Pickens. Comrade Randall's term of Navy service expired in 1862, and he was honorably discharged therefrom.

After remaining at home for a short time, he enlisted August 8, 1862, as a Private in Capt. Betton's company, K. of the 13th Regiment, N. H. Volunteers, for a term of three years, and participated in nearly every engagement that the regiment was in. At the battles of Fredericksburg, Suffolk, at Bermuda Hundred, the ten days fight at Coal [Cold] Harbor, at the capture of Battery 5 in front of Petersburg, and many other engagements, the tall and conspicuous form of Charles W. Randall, could be seen at the right of the company; and yet there were more jewels to be added to his crown of honor, for in the famous charge and capture of Fort Harrison on Sept 29, 1864, comrade Randall bore his part of that terrible battle.

On the day following the capture of the fort, and while the regiment was lying behind shallow breastworks composed of two logs, from which the rebels had been repulsed by our scanty forces in three successive charges, he was struck by a bullet, which entered the body just back of, and below the right arm, making a very bad wound, which was pronounced mortal. Notwithstanding his injury his courage never failed him, and he remarked to his comrade, First Sergeant B. F. Winn, that he wished for one more shot before leaving the field, he succeeded in loading and firing his rifle, and then made his way to the rear as best he could. His wound was probed for the bullet, but without success, and his condition was pronounced hopeless. A strong constitution and a persistent courage which nothing daunted, kept him up, however, and he was restored to partial health.

Our comrade was a constant sufferer from the effects of the rebel bullet which he carried for twenty-three years, and yet his spirit remained unbroken till the last, and when his brave soul left the poor shrunken body, encumbered with rebel lead, there passed away as brave a soldier as ever wore the blue.

Comrade Randall joined Storer Post, G. A. R., May 27, 1881, where he remained a respected member, and his death adds one more to the silent roll-call."

Soldiers Memorial, 1888.

Randall, Reuben S.—War 1812.

Rice, William A.—83rd N. Y.

"Private, Co. D. Enlisted and Mustered in May 27, 1861, for the war. Promoted to Sergeant, October 5, 1861. Discharged at Manassas Junction, Va., July 3, 1862, for disability.

The 83rd N. Y. was formerly the 9th Regiment N. Y. State Militia."

Adjutant General's Records, N. Y.

He was a member of the 9th Regiment N. Y. State Militia, and went to the front with that Regiment (then the 83rd N. Y.) in 1861. He died at Chicago, Illinois, October 9, 1866.

Richards, Henry L.—2d U. S. Sharpshooters.

Henry Lakeman Richards.

"Born Feb. 19, 1824, Died at Gettysburg, Penn., July 4, 1863." *Stone.*

"Private, Co. F. Residence or assignment, Portsmouth. Date of Muster, Nov. 26, 1861, for 3 years. Promoted to Sergeant. Wounded at Antietam, Md., Sept. 17, 1862. Killed at Gettysburg, Pa., July 2 [See above], 1863."

Adjutant General's Records, N. H.

"Late Henry L. Richards.—It pains us to say that this noble hearted man is no more. At the commencement of the rebellion he offered his services in defence of his country. Though possessing sterling ability, he sought no high position, but only that in which he was confident of being most useful. When requested to take a commission, his reply was, 'No —I had rather be a good soldier than a poor officer.'

When the company of Sharpshooters was forming at Concord, he went on foot to that place from Portsmouth, was examined, accepted, and he returned home in the same way, to fit up for his departure. After an absence with the army of fourteen months, in which time he was exposed in several engagements, he came home wounded in November [1862] last.

As soon as his health would permit he again joined the army, on the Rappahannock, and on the 2d of July [1863], at the battle of Gettysburg, was severely wounded in his knee by a minnie ball. After remaining on the ground all night, he was taken up and carried to the hospital, where amputation was performed, while under the influence of chloroform, from the effects of which he did not revive. His age was 38 [39]. His remains will probably reach here in a few days, and the performance of the last sad rites will bring feelings of heartfelt sorrow to our whole community.

And now, and in all future time, as those who knew him well pass under the shade which is just beginning to be made by the long range of trees in Auburn street, they will be reminded of the one who selected and with his own hand placed them there to cheer the passage to the cemetery—and the name of the noble Richards will be as green in their memory as the leaves which every returning spring will renew."

Portsmouth Journal, July 18, 1863.

Soon after the death of Henry L. Richards, the name of Auburn street was changed to Richards' avenue, in memory of him.

Ridge, Charles—2nd N. H.

Ridge, Thomas W.—U. S. Navy.

"Son of Charles and Susan Ridge." *Stone.*

Rogers, Joseph W.—2nd N. H.

"Private, Co. K. Residence or assignment, Portsmouth. Date of Muster, June 8, 1861, for 3 years. Discharged for disability, at Budd's Ferry, Md., May 31, 1862."

Adjutant General's Records, N. H.

Rokes, Lincoln—10th N. H.

Enlisted as "Lincoln Roakes."

"Lincoln Rokes." *Stone.*

"Private, Co. G. Residence or assignment, Portsmouth. Date of Muster, Sept. 1, 1862, for 3 years. Discharged for disability, March 25, 1863."

Adjutant General's Records, N. H.

Ross, Charles H.—U. S. Navy.

"Charles Ross." *Stone.*

Russell, John—U. S. Navy.

Rutter, Thomas—10th N. H.

"Private, Co. G. Residence, Portsmouth. Date of Muster, Sept. 4, 1862, for 3 years. Discharged for disability, June 20, 1864."

Adjutant General's Records, N. H.

Salisbury, Wm. Henry—. . . .

"Born at Warren, R. I. . . . Died at Portsmouth, N. H." *Stone.*

Salmon, Thomas—U. S. Navy.

Member Storer Post, G. A. R.

Second Class Fireman, U. S. Steamer "Kearsarge."

"Fireman. Birthplace, Ireland. Enlisted Feb. 4, 1862, U. S. Steamer 'Kearsarge.' Discharged Nov. 29, 1864, expiration of enlistment." *Post Records.*

One of the crew of the U. S. Steamer "Kearsarge" when she destroyed the "Alabama," off Cherbourg, France, June 19, 1864. See record of Mark G. Ham.

Sawyer, George—1st Mass.

"Wounded at battle of Wilderness 1864. Died at Portsmouth, N. H."

Stone.

"Private, Co. G. Residence, Roxbury, Mass. Enlisted May 23, 1861. Date of Muster, May 23, 1861, for 3 years. Promoted to Corporal. Mustered out May 25, 1864, expiration of service."

Adjutant General's Records, Mass.

Sawyer, Samuel—23rd Mass.

"Born in Saco, Me. Died in Auburn, N. H." *Stone.*

"Private, Co. K. Residence, Franklin, Mass. Enlisted Sept. 25, 1861. Date of Muster, Sept. 28, 1861, for 3 years. Discharged for disability, June 11, 1862."

Adjutant General's Records, Mass.

Saxton, Mortimer F.—30th Mass.

"Mortimer Faxon Saxton, born at Weathersfield, Vt. . . . Died at New Orleans, La., in the service of his Country. . . . He rests in southern soil."

Stone.

"Private, Co. H. Residence, Boston. Enlisted Dec. 1, 1861. Date of Muster, Dec. 1, 1861, for 3 years. Died at New Orleans, La., Oct. 11, 1862."

Adjutant General's Records, Mass.

Seaver, John W.—47th Mass.

"A dutiful son and loving husband."

Stone.

"Private, Co. F. Residence, Boston. Enlisted ———. Date of Muster, Oct. 9, 1862, for 9 months. Discharged for disability, Nov. 28, 1862."

Adjutant General's Records, Mass.

Seavey, Joseph J.—19th Mass.

Member Storer Post, G. A. R.

"Private, Co. F. Residence, Gloucester, Mass. Enlisted Aug. 6, 1861. Date of Muster, Aug. 28, 1861, for 3 years. Reënlisted Dec. 21, 1863. Wagoner. Mustered out June 30, 1865."

Adjutant General's Records, Mass.

"Birthplace, Portsmouth."

Post Records.

Seymour, Frank—4th N. Y. Art.

"Private, Co. L. Enrolled and mustered Dec. 15, 1863. Commissioned 2nd Lieutenant, April 14, 1864, with rank from March 22, 1864. Commissioned 1st Lieutenant, January 31, 1865, with rank from January 1, 1865. Mustered out with Company, Sept. 26, 1865."

Adjutant General's Records, N. Y.

Shapley, John H.—1st N. H. Cav.

"Killed at Waynesboro, Va." *Stone.*

"Private, Troop M, N. H. Battalion, 1st N. E. Cavalry. Residence, Rye. Date of Muster, Dec. 24, 1861, for 3 years. Promoted to Corporal. Captured near Middleburg, Va., June 18, 1863. Paroled 1863. Rëenlisted, Corporal, Troop M. Residence, Rye. Date of Muster, Jan. 5, 1864, for 3 years. Battalion reorganized as 1st Regiment N. H. Cavalry, March 1864. Sergeant, Troop M. Promoted to 1st Sergeant. Killed at Waynesboro, Va., Sept 28 1864."

Adjutant General's Records, N. H.

Shapley, Robert P.—1st N. H. Cav.

"Died at Darnestown, Md." *Stone.*

"Private, Troop M, N. H. Battalion, 1st N. E. Cavalry. Residence, Rye. Date of Muster, Dec. 24, 1861, for 3 years. Promoted Sergeant, Jan. 28, 1862 Captured near Middleburg, Va., June 18, 1863. Paroled, 1863. Rëenlisted, Troop M. Residence, Rye. Date of Muster, Jan. 5, 1864, for 3 years. Appointed 1st Sergeant. Battalion rëorganized as 1st N. H. Cavalry. March, 1864. 1st Sergeant, Troop M. Promoted to 1st Lieutenant, Troop M. Date of Commission, July 15, 1864. Died of disease at Darnestown, Md., June 2, 1865."

Adjutant General's Records, N. H.

Shaw, John—16th N. H.

"Private, Co K. Residence, Portsmouth. Date of Muster, Nov. 11, 1862, for 9 months. Mustered out Aug. 20, 1863."

Adjutant General's Records, N. H.

Sherburne, John C.—10th N. H.

John Colbath Sherburne.

"Sherburne." *Stone.*

"Private, Co. G. Residence, Portsmouth. Date of Muster, Sept. 4, 1862, for 3 years. Discharged for disability Jan. 17, 1863."

Adjutant General's Records, N. H.

Shillaber, Robert E.—1st N. H. Cav.

"Private, Troop M, N. H. Battalion, 1st N. E. Cavalry. Residence, Portsmouth. Date of Muster, Jan. 8, 1862, for 3 years. Promoted to Corporal, Jan. 28, 1862. Rëenlisted, Private, Troop M. Residence, Portsmouth. Date of Muster, Jan. 5, 1864, for 3 years. Battalion rëorganized as 1st Regiment, N. H. Cavalry, March 1864. Private, Troop M. Transferred to Troop A, July 1, 1864. Promoted to Troop Quartermaster Sergeant. Reduced to Private May 1. 1865. Discharged for disability June 12, 1865."

Adjutant General's Records, N. H.

Shock, Thomas A.—U. S. Navy.

"Died Jan. 11, 1873." *Stone.*

"Third Assistant Engineer, 6 February, 1851. Second Assistant Engineer, 21 May, 1853. First Assistant Engineer, 26 June, 1856. Chief Engineer, 6 December, 1860. Died 21 January [See above], 1873."

Hamersly's General Navy Register.

"Died at Boston, Mass., January 21 [See above], 1873."

Navy Register, 1874.

Shuttleworth, Wm.—U. S. M. C.

Sides, George L.—13th N. H.

"Private, Co. K. Residence or assignment, Portsmouth. Date of Muster, Sept. 20, 1862, for 3 years. Mustered out June 21, 1865 "

Adjutant General's Records, N. H.

Small, Robert—U. S. M. C.

Smart, George E.—U. S. Navy.

Second Class Fireman, U. S. Steamer "Kearsarge."

One of the crew of the U. S. Steamer "Kearsarge" when she destroyed the "Alabama," off Cherbourg, France, June 19, 1864. See record of Mark G. Ham.

Smith, James—3rd U. S. Art.

Smith, William—Mex. War.

"A veteran of the Mexican War."

Stone.

Snow, James B.—U. S. Navy.

Spalding, Champion—War 1812.

"Lieut. Champin Spalding, Jr."

Stone.

"1st Lieut , Capt. James M. Warner's Company, 2nd Regiment, N. H. Detached Militia. Residence, Plainfield. Enlisted Sept. 25, 1814, for 60 days. Died Oct. 12, 1814."

Adjutant General's Report, N. H., 1868.

"Champion Spalding, born January 2, 1788, died October 28, 1814."—"He was in the army during the war of 1812, and died at a fort [See below] near Portsmouth, N. H." He was the son of Deacon Champion Spalding, of Claremont, N. H.

Spalding Memorial, Boston, 1872.

He died "at the Plains. . . . He belonged to the detached militia stationed there, and on Sunday last [Oct. 30, 1814], his remains were brought into town and interred with military honors."

N. H. Gazette, Nov. 1, 1814.

Spalding, Lyman G.—U. S. Navy.

Lyman Greenleafe Spalding was Captain's Clerk of the U. S Steamer "Augusta." Commander Enoch Greenleafe Parrott (afterwards Rear Admiral) commanding, for about twelve months in the years 1861 and 1862; took part in the capture of Port Royal, S. C., by Rear Admiral DuPont, November 7 1861, and afterwards served on the blockade of Charleston, S. C.

"Midshipman, 26 September, 1862. Graduated June, 1866 Resigned 16 June, 1866. Master, 28 June, 1871. Lieutenant, 10 July, 1875. Killed by explosion of a torpedo at Newport, R. I, 29 August, 1881."

Hamersly's General Navy Register.

"Born in New Hampshire. Entered Naval Academy, July, 1862 [See above]; graduated as Midshipman, June, 1866; out of the service five years; reappointed and commissioned as Master, June 28, 1871; 'Canonicus' (ironclad), North Atlantic Station, 1871-2; 'Yantic,' Asiatic Squadron, 1872-5 Commissioned Lieutenant, July 10, 1875; sick leave, 1876; 'Enterprise,' special service, surveying Amazon River, 1877; and same vessel, European Squadron, 1878-80."

Hamersly's Naval Encyclopedia.

"The terrible accident in Newport harbor on Monday last," August 29, 1881, resulting in the instant death by the explosion of a torpedo, of Lieut. Commander Benjamin Long Edes and Lieutenant Lyman Greenleafe Spalding of the United States Navy, "specially receives the profound sympathy and regard of this community.

A resident of this city, and a Portsmouth boy by birth, Lieutenant Spalding was recognized and valued by those who knew him, as a man of estimable character and honorable ambition. The descendant of one of our best known families, he was born January 1, 1845, and was admitted to the Naval School at Newport, September 25 [26], 1862. He was graduated thence and entered the United States Navy [See above], receiving the commission of Master, June 28, 1871, and of Lieutenant July 10, 1875.

Although comparatively a young man, it was the good fortune of Lieutenant Spalding to have rendered very acceptable services to the Government upon various occasions, among which is specially to be noted his last cruise in the United States steamer 'Enterprise,' detailed upon survey duty along the coast of South America, and closed in May, 1880."

"It may truthfully be said of Lieutenant Spalding, that he honored the uniform which he wore, in discharging the duties which devolved upon him with a high sense of conscientiousness and fidelity. Frank and straightforward in disposition, he was possessed of many noble qualities of head and heart, which endeared him to those who knew him best."

"We voice the general sentiment of our citizens in expressing the sorrow of this community, and its sympathy for his bereaved family. In his untimely end, Portsmouth is deprived of one ever attached to its welfare, and the United States Navy sustains the loss of a trusted and promising officer and gentleman."

Portsmouth Journal, Sept. 3, 1881.

Spinney, George A.—6 Inf. & 1 Cav. Mass.

"In memory of
George A Spinney,
of Co. D,
1st Mass. Cav.
Fell at the battle of Aldie, Va.,
June 17, 1863,
Aged 25 years.
He was formerly a member of the Mass. 6th, who were the first to answer to their Country's call.
He was beloved by all who knew him and still lives in our hearts.
He sleeps in southern soil."

Stone.

"Private, Co. K, 6th Mass. Infantry. Residence, Boston. Enlisted ——. Date of Muster, April 22, 1861, for 3 months. Discharged Aug. 2, 1861, expiration of service.

Private, Troop D, 1st Mass. Cavalry. Residence, South Boston. Enlisted Sept. 21, 1861. Date of Muster, Sept. 23, 1861, for 3 years. Killed at Aldie, Va., June 17, 1863."

Adjutant General's Records, Mass.

Spinney, Horace S.—13th N. H.

"Private, Co. K. Residence or assignment, Portsmouth. Date of Muster, Sept. 20, 1862, for 3 years. Mustered out June 21, 1865."

Adjutant General's Records, N. H.

Stack, Michael F.—U. S. Navy.

"Mich'l Stack." *Stone.*

Staples, Samuel—57th Mass.

"Private, Co. D. Residence, Medford, Mass. Enlisted Jan. 11, 1864. Date of Muster, Feb. 9, 1864. for 3 years. Mustered out July 30, 1865"

Adjutant General's Records, Mass.

Stearns, James—5th N. H.

"Corporal, Co. K. Residence or assignment, Portsmouth. Date of Muster, Oct. 12, 1861, for 3 years. Discharged for disability, at New York City, Jan. 21, 1863."

Adjutant General's Records, N. H.

"Birthplace, Portsmouth."

Post Records.

He was for some time a member of Storer Post, but not at the time of his death.

Storer, George W.—U. S. Navy.

"George Washington Storer.
Rear Admiral, U. S. Navy,
Born May 1, 1789,
Died January 8, 1864."

Stone.

"Navy Department,
Washington, D. C., Jan. 13, 1864.

The Department announces to the Navy and Marine Corps, the death of Rear Admiral George W. Storer. He died at his residence in Portsmouth, N. H., on the morning of the 8th inst., after an honorable career in the Navy of nearly fifty-five years. Rear Admiral Storer was correct in his deportment, attached to his profession, and devoted to his country. As an officer in the Navy he has served faithfully, and has filled with credit many important positions both ashore and afloat.

As a mark of respect to his memory, it is hereby directed that at the Portsmouth, N. H. Navy Yard the flags be hoisted at half-mast and thirteen minute-guns be fired at meridian on the day after the receipt hereof.

Gideon Welles,
Secretary of the Navy."

"Midshipman, 16 January, 1809. Lieutenant, 24 July, 1813. Commander, 24 April, 1828. Captain, 9 February, 1837. [Retired 21 December, 1861—See below.] Rear Admiral on Retired List, 16 July, 1862. Died 8 January, 1864."

Hamersly's General Navy Register.

"Storer, George Washington, naval officer, born in Portsmouth, N. H., in 1789; died there 8 Jan. 1864. He entered the Navy as a Midshipman, 16 Jan. 1809, and was commissioned a Lieutenant, 24 July, 1813. He served in the ship 'Independence' on the Mediterranean station in 1815-16, commanded the schooner 'Lynx' on the New England coast and in the Gulf of Mexico in 1817, cruised in the frigates 'Congress' and 'Java' in the West Indies in 1818-19, and in the frigate 'Constitution' in the Mediterranean in 1820-4. He was commissioned Master Commandant, 24 April, 1828, and Captain 9 Feb., 1837, commanded the receiving-ship 'Constellation' at Boston in 1839, the frigate 'Potomac,' of the Brazil station, in 1840-2, the Navy Yard at Portsmouth in 1843-6, and was the Commander-in-Chief of the Brazil squadron in 1847-50. He was on leave and served as member of boards, president of the board of inquiry, and other duty in 1851-4. In 1855-7 he was Governor of the Naval Asylum at Philadelphia. He was retired, 21 Dec. 1861, on account of age, and promoted to Rear Admiral on the Retired list, 16 July, 1862. In 1861-2 he served on special duty in Brooklyn, after which he was unemployed for one year."

Appleton's Cyclopedia of American Biography.

It is related in Brewster's "Rambles about Portsmouth," 1st series, pages 254 and 266, that during Washington's visit to Portsmouth in 1789, he called, Tuesday forenoon, November 3rd, on Mrs. Tobias Lear, the mother of his private secretary, Col. Tobias Lear, then living near the east end of Hunking street, and "in the south-west parlor, he was introduced to and cordially greeted every member of the family—the venerable mother, her children and her grandchildren."

Among the grandchildren a babe is presented, son of Samuel Storer, a dry goods merchant of Portsmouth, then residing in the same house, "who has been christened 'George Washington.' The President places his hand gently upon the infant's head, and expresses the wish that he may 'be a better man than the one whose name he bears.'"

This child was George Washington Storer—and as his name is proudly borne by Storer Post, it is particularly worthy of remembrance that he is one of the very few men of whom it could be said "that they have thus been under the hand and received thus the personal blessing of our country's father."

Storer, Robert B.—Mex. War.

"Robert Blunt Storer, Midshipman, U. S. N." *Stone.*

"Midshipman, 4 November, 1841. Died at Sea, 4 July, 1847."
Hamersly's General Navy Register.

"Died—July 4 [1847], on board the U. S. Frigate 'Raritan,' Midshipman Robert B. Storer, son of Capt. Geo. W. Storer [U. S. Navy], of this town, aged 22. Mr. Storer was on his return voyage after three years' absence, and the tidings of his death came by the very mail by which his friends were expecting news by his own hand of his safe arrival at Norfolk."

"U. S. Frigate 'Raritan,'
July 22, 1847.

Sir:

It is with deep regret that I inform the Department of the demise of Midshipman Robert B. Storer, who died of fever on the passage to the United States on the 4th instant. He was buried at sea, with the ceremony due to his rank.

Mr. Storer had been attached to the 'Cumberland' under my command; and at his request was transferred to this ship, that he might lend his services to the war in whatever quarter they might be needed.

The ability and zeal with which he discharged his duties, and his exemplary, amiable and moral deportment, rendered him a great favorite on board. It will be a melancholy satisfaction to his relatives to know that every attention and kindness was extended to him during his illness, and that his shipmates feel the bereavement in common with his nearest kindred.

I have the honor to be, very respectfully,
F. Forrest, Captain.

Hon. John Y. Mason,
Secretary of the Navy."

Portsmouth Journal, August 7, 1847.

"The U. S. Frigate 'Raritan' arrived at Norfolk, Va., from Vera Cruz, Mexico, July 22, 1847."
Emmons' Navy of the United States.

Stott, George—13th N. H.

Member of Storer Post, G. A. R.

"Private, Co. K. Residence or assignment, Portsmouth. Date of Muster, Sept. 20, 1862, for 3 years. Discharged for disability at Portsmouth, Va, April 16, 1864."
Adjutant General's Records, N. H.

"Birthplace, England."
Post Records.

"He was born in Rochdale, England, January 4, 1817. In 1844 he came to this country and set up the machinery for the mill at Ballardvale, Mass., and two years later came to this city and arranged the machinery for the old Kearsarge mills." He was foreman of the spinning room of the Kearsarge mills for the twenty years ending in 1868, and afterwards engaged in the grocery business.

"Early in the war he enlisted in Captain Betton's Co. of the 13th N. H. Volunteers, and served bravely in all of the engagements. Two sons, John W. and Robert A., were also in the service and served with bravery."
Portsmouth Daily Eve. Post, June 24, 1892.

Stott, Robert A.—17th & 2nd N. H.

Member Storer Post, G. A. R.
"Son of George and Mary Stott."
Stone.

"Private, Co. B, 17th N. H. Residence or assignment, Portsmouth. Date of Muster, Nov. 13, 1862, for 9 months. Consolidated with Co. K, 2nd N. H. V., April 16, 1863.

Private, Co. K, 2nd N. H. Recruit. Transferred from 17th N. H. V., April 16, 1863. Mustered out October 9, 1863."
Adjutant General's Records, N. H.

"Birthplace, Ballardvale, Mass."
Post Records.

Stringer, Joseph W.—U. S. Navy.

"Son of John and Elizabeth Stringer."
Stone.

Sullivan, Peter—10th N. H.

"Private, Co. G. Residence or assignment, Portsmouth. Date of Muster, Sept. 5, 1862, for 3 years. Mustered out June 16, 1865."
Adjutant General's Records, N. H.

Sweeney, Barney—N. H. H. Art.

"Private, 1st Co. Residence, Columbia. Date of Muster, May 26, 1863, for 3 years. Died at Fort Constitution, near Portsmouth, N. H., Oct. 21, 1863."
Adjutant General's Records, N. H.

Talham, Charles A.—2nd N. H.

"Charles Alfred Talham."

"Tread softly: this is hallowed ground;
Come with a noiseless tread
For underneath this lonely mound
A brave true heart lies dead.
A brave true heart as ever beat
In mortal breast lies here
Let us sit down awhile and weep
O'er his lone grave so dear.
Yes weep; but not for his dear sake,
Who sleeps so peacefully—
They who sleep calmly in their graves
Are better off than we.

And here he lies insensible
Alike to pain or mirth:
Ah, how much valor when he died
And virtue fled from earth.
His sufferings were terrible,
Before he went to sleep,
But he will never suffer more
His slumber is so deep.
O, never bitterer tears were wept,
Than those I shed for him
His dark eyes once were bright with joy,
But sorrow made them dim."

Stone.

"Private, Co. D. Residence or assignment, Portsmouth. Date of Muster, June 1, 1861, for 3 years. Died of disease at Brooklyn, N. Y., Sept. 27, 1862."

Adjutant General's Records, N. H.

Taylor, Alfred—U. S. Navy.

"Midshipman, 1 January, 1825. Passed Midshipman, 4 June, 1831. Lieutenant, 9 February, 1837. Commander, 14 September, 1855. Captain, 16 July, 1862. Commodore, 27 September, 1866. Rear-Admiral, 29 January, 1872. Retired list, 23 May, 1872."

Hamersly's General Navy Register.

"Died at Washington, D. C., April 19, 1891." *Navy Register, 1892.*

"Appointed Midshipman, 1825; Mediterranean Squadron, 1826-9; Pacific Squadron, 1830-2.

Promoted to Passed Midshipman, June 4, 1831; Navy Yard, Portsmouth, 1833; Navy Yard, Boston, 1834; Brazil Squadron, 1835-6.

Commissioned as Lieutenant, February 9, 1837; sloop 'Cyane,' Mediterranean Squadron, 1840-2; Navy Yard, Washington, 1843; sloop 'Boston,' Brazil Squadron, 1845-6; attached to frigate 'Cumberland,' Home Squadron, during Mexican War; Navy Yard, Washington, 1848-51; steam-sloop 'Mississippi,' East India Squadron, 1853-5

Commissioned as Commander, September 14, 1855; commanding rendezvous, New York, 1856-8; commanding sloop 'Saratoga,' 1861.

Commissioned as Captain, 1862; Navy Yard, Boston, 1862-5; commanding flagship 'Susquehanna,' Brazil Squadron, 1866.

Commissioned as Commodore, Septem- 27 1866; Light-House Inspector, 1868-72.

Commissioned as Rear-Admiral, January 29, 1872."

Hamersly's Naval Records, 1878.

Rear-Admiral Alfred Taylor, U. S. Navy, "was born in Fairfax county, Va., in 1810, and entered the navy as Midshipman in 1825. He reached the grade of Lieutenant in 1837, and in the Mexican war, during the blockade of Vera Cruz and the other naval operations along the Mexican coast he served with the frigate 'Cumberland.' From 1849 [1848] to 1851 he was detailed to duty in the Washington navy yard. He was on duty in the steamer 'Mississippi' with Com. Perry's expedition to Japan in 1853-5. In the latter year he was promoted to the grade of Commander, and when the civil war broke out was stationed on the coast of Africa, in charge of the sloop 'Saratoga.' In 1862 he became a Captain, and was attached to the Boston navy yard, remaining there until 1865. He was promoted to Commodore and subsequently, in 1872, to the grade of Rear-Admiral, and was retired soon after. Rear-Admiral Taylor married a daughter of Major [General] Justin Dimick, U. S. A., of this city."

Portsmouth Journal, April 25, 1891.

Taylor, George—13th N. H.

"Private, Co. K. Residence or assignment, Rye. Date of Muster, Sept. 20, 1862, for 3 years. Promoted to Corporal. Wounded severely at Chapin's Farm, Va., Sept. 29, 1864. Discharged for disability at Manchester, N. H., May 3, 1865."

Adjutant General's Records, N. H.

Tetherly, Andrew—U. S. Navy.

"Son of John S. and Thankful Tetherly." *Stone.*

Thacher, Joseph H.—16th N. H.

Member of Storer Post, G. A. R.

"Captain, Co. K. Residence, Portsmouth. Commissioned Nov. 4, 1862. Mustered out Aug. 20, 1863, expiration of service."

Adjutant General's Records, N. H.

"Born at Biddeford, Maine, February 10, 1825. He was the son of Henry Savage Thacher and Elizabeth Haven Wardrobe, and grandson of Hon. George Thacher of Biddeford, member of the first U. S. Congress, and for many years Judge of the Supreme Court of Massachusetts, when Maine was a part of that State.

He was educated at Hopkinton academy, Hopkinton, N. H., and learned the profession of chemist and druggist, first establishing himself in business in Boston, but removing to this city [Portsmouth] about 1846, and continuing in business until May 1888, when ill health obliged him to retire.

He served as Captain, Co. K. 16th N. H. Volunteers, in the war of the Rebellion, was in General Banks' department, and present at the memorable attack upon and surrender of Port Hudson.

He was a successful merchant, a master of his chosen profession, an excellent citizen, and an honest, independent, but singularly modest and self-contained man, and one who made many friends, and retained every one he ever made.

Died in Portsmouth January 5, 1892."

Soldiers Memorial, 1892.

Thompson, . . .—3rd U. S. Art.

His full name is not known.

Thompson, Thomas—Rev. War.

"Died.—In this town [Portsmouth, N. H.] on Wednesday last [February 22, 1809], Thomas Thompson, Esq., President of the N. H. Fire and Marine Insurance Company, in the 68th year of his age."

N. H. Gazette, Tuesday, February 28, 1809.

The house, now the residence of Mark H. Wentworth, Esq., No. 34 Pleasant street, Portsmouth, was "built by Capt. Thomas Thompson in 1784. Capt. Thompson was one of the first naval officers commissioned by the Continental Congress. He commanded the frigate 'Raleigh,' and afterwards (1785) was Colonel of a regiment of Artillery. The house was long the residence of Dr. Josiah Dwight, who married a daughter of Capt. Thompson." *Portsmouth Guide Book.*

In the "Travels" of the Marquis de Chastelleux, who was in Portsmouth, in 1782, it is said of Captain Thompson, that he "was born in England: he is a good seaman and an excellent shipbuilder, and is besides a sensible man, greatly attached to his new country, which it is only fifteen years since he adopted."

Rambles About Portsmouth, Second Series.

"In the 'Journals of Congress,' under date of Thursday, June 6th, 1776, is the following: 'Resolved that Thomas Thompson be appointed Captain of the frigate built in New Hampshire.' And again under date of Oct. 10th, 1776, we find a second commission as Captain in the Navy of the United States granted him, making him number six on the list of Captains."

"The following is a copy of the Commission of Captain Thompson of the Frigate 'Raleigh' [dated Oct 10, 1776]:

In Congress.

The Delegates of the United States of New Hampshire, Massachusetts-Bay, Rhode-Island, Connecticut, New York, New-Jersey, Pennsylvania, Delaware, Maryland, Virginia, North Carolina and Georgia—

To

Thomas Thompson, Esquire.

*We, reposing especial Trust and Confidence in your Patriotism, Valor, Conduct and Fidelity, Do, by these Presents, constitute and appoint you to be Captain in the Navy of the United States of North America, fitted out for the defence of American Liberty, and for repelling every hostile Invasion thereof. You are therefore carefully and diligently to discharge the Duty of Captain by doing and performing all manner of Things thereunto belonging.

And we do strictly charge and require all Officers, Marines and Seamen under your command to be obedient to your Orders as Captain. And you are to observe and follow such Orders and Directions from Time to Time, as you shall receive from this or a future Congress.

Dated at Philadelphia, October 10th, 1776.

By order of the Congress.

John Hancock,
President.

(Attest.) Chas. Thompson, Sect'y.

*Number Six. The number of Commission determines the rank. John Hancock,
Pres't."

After the Revolution the State of New Hampshire "appointed him Colonel of Artillery. His commission as Colonel is signed by Governor John Langdon, and is dated the 11th day of August, 1785.

Captain Thompson died at Portsmouth, in 1809."

"List of Officers and Petty Officers of the U. S. Frigate 'Raleigh', August, 1775 [1777]."

Names.	*Rank.*	*Where belonging.*
Thomas Thompson,	Commander,	Portsmouth.
Peter Shores,	1st Lieut.	"
Josiah Shackford,	2d "	"
Hopley Yeaton,	4th "	"
Thomas Manning,	Master,	"
John Yeaton,	Mate,	"
Robert Curtis,	"	"
John Adams,	Purser,	"
John Jackson,	Surgeon,	"
John Quinn,	Surg. Mate,	Kittery.
George J. Osborn,	Capt. Marines,	Exeter.
Stephen Meads,	1st Lt. Marines,	New York.
Nath'l Thwing,	2d " "	Boston.
William Bray,	Boatswain,	Portsmouth.
William Cambridge,	Gunner,	England.
Simeon Fernald,	Carpenter,	Portsmouth.
Benj. Dam,	Sailmaker,	Kittery.
John Frost,	Midshipman,	Portsmouth.
Sam. McClintock,	"	"
Rich'd Littlefield,	"	"
Dan'l Durgan,	"	"
Dan'l Lang,	"	"
Rich'd Langdon,	Capt's Clerk,	"
Sam'l Parcher,	Steward,	New Hampshire.
Wm. Ward,	Coxswain,	"
Robert Whipple,	Armorer,	Portsmouth.
Robert Cockran,	Cooper,	"
James Furlong,	Boat's Mate,	"
Henry Williams,	"	"
Philip McCann,	"	Newburyport.
Wm. Stevens,	Cook,	"
Henry Cate,	Mast. at Arms,	Portsmouth.
Francis Little,	Gun's Mate,	"
Nicholas Bufford,	Yeoman,	"
Ebenezer Pray,	Carp's Mate,	"

Mathias Bell,	Boat's Yeoman,	Portsmouth
Joseph Clements,	Capt's Steward,	"
Thomas Passmore,	Quartermaster,	"
John Mendum,	"	"
Wm. Mendum,	"	"
Peter Meserve,	"	"
John Fernald,	"	"

Fentress' History Portsmouth, N. H., Navy Yard.

In August, 1777, "the 'Raleigh,' a fine twelve-pounder frigate, that had been constructed in New Hampshire, under the law of 1775, was enabled to get to sea for the first time. She was commanded by Captain Thompson, the officer who appears as sixth on the list, and sailed in company with the 'Alfred,' 24, Captain Hinman. These two ships went to sea, short of men, bound to France, where military stores were in waiting to be transported to America.

The 'Raleigh' and 'Alfred' had a good run off the coast, and they made several prizes of little value during the first few days of their passage. On the 2d of September they overtook and captured a snow, called the 'Nancy,' which had been left by the outward bound Windward Island fleet the previous day. Ascertaining from his prisoners the position of the West Indiamen, Captain Thompson made sail in chase. The fleet was under the charge of the 'Camel', 'Druid,' 'Weasel,' and 'Grasshopper,' the first of which is said to have had an armament of twelve pounders. The following day, or September 3d, 1777, the 'Raleigh' made the convoy from her mast-heads, and by sunset was near enough to ascertain that there were sixty sail, as well as the positions of the men-of-war. Captain Thompson had got the signals of the fleet from his prize, and he now signalled the 'Alfred,' as if belonging to the convoy. After dark he spoke his consort, and directed her commander to keep near him, it being his intention to run in among the enemy, and to lay the commodore aboard. At this time, the two American ships were to windward, but nearly astern.

In the course of the night the wind shifted to the northward, and the convoy hauled by the wind, bringing the American ships to leeward. At daylight the wind had freshened, and it became necessary to carry more sail than the 'Alfred' (a tender-sided ship) could bear. Here occurred one of those instances of the unfortunate consequences which must always follow the employment of vessels of unequal qualities in the same squadron, or the employment of officers not trained in the same high school. The 'Alfred' would not bear her canvas, and while the 'Raleigh' fetched handsomely into the fleet, under double-reefed topsails, the former fell to leeward more than a league. Captain Thompson did not dare to shorten sail, lest his character might be suspected, and despairing of being supported by the 'Alfred,' he stood boldly in among the British ships alone, and hove-to his ship in order to permit the merchantmen astern to draw more ahead of him.

When his plan was laid, Captain Thompson filled away, and stood directly through the convoy, luffing up towards the vessel of war that was most to windward. In doing this he spoke several of the merchantmen, giving them orders how to steer, as if belonging himself to the fleet, and repeating all the commodore's signals. Up to this moment the 'Raleigh' appears to have escaped detection, nor had she any signs of preparation about her, as her guns were housed, and her ports lowered.

Having obtained a weatherly position, the 'Raleigh' now ran along-side of the vessel-of-war, and when within pistol-shot, she hauled up her courses, run out her guns, set her ensign, and commanded the enemy to strike. So completely was this vessel taken by surprise, that the order threw her into great confusion, and even her sails got aback. The 'Raleigh' seized this favorable moment to pour in a broadside, which was feebly returned. The enemy were soon driven from their guns, and the 'Raleigh' fired twelve broadsides into the English ship in twenty minutes, scarcely receiving a shot in return. A heavy swell rendered the aim uncertain, but it was evident that the British vessel suffered severely, and this the more so, as she was of inferior force.

A squall had come on, and at first it shut in the two ships engaged. When it cleared away, the convoy was seen steering in all directions, in the utmost confusion, but the vessels of war, with several heavy well-armed West Indiamen, tacked and hauled up for the 'Raleigh,' leaving no doubt of their intentions to engage. The frigate lay by her adversary until the other vessels were so near, that it became absolutely necessary to quit her, and then she ran to leeward and joined the 'Alfred.' Here she shortened sail, and waited for the enemy to come down, but it being dark, the British commodore tacked and hauled in among his convoy again. The 'Raleigh' and 'Alfred' kept near this fleet for several days, but no provocation could induce the vessels of war to come out of it, and it was finally abandoned.

The ship engaged by the 'Raleigh,' proved to be the 'Druid,' 20, Captain Carteret. She was much cut up, and the official report of her commander made her loss six killed and twenty-six wounded. Of the latter, five died soon after the action, and among the wounded was her commander. The 'Druid' was unable to pursue the voyage, and returned to England.

In this affair, Captain Thompson discovered a proper spirit, for he might easily have cut out of the fleet half a dozen merchantmen, but he appears to have acted on the principle that vessels of war should first seek vessels of war. The 'Raleigh' had three men killed and wounded in the engagement, but otherwise sustained little injury."

Cooper's Naval History.

The "Raleigh", 32, built at Portsmouth, in 1776, under the superintendence of Captain Thomas Thompson, was captured by the British in 1778. Capt. John Barry was then in command.

Towle, George W.—10th N. H.

"To the memory of
George William Towle,
Born in Epping, N. H., Sept. 19, 1810,
Died in Chicago, Ill., April 20, 1887.
Captain Tenth New Hampshire
Infantry, in the war for the
Union. Action at Orleans, Va., Nov.
5, 1862. Battle of Fredericksburg,
Dec. 13, 1862. Siege of Suffolk,
April 10, 1863 Assault on Battery,
Nansemond river, Va., April 19,
1863. Siege of Petersburg, 1864.
Campaign before Richmond, 1864 5.
'Without a sign, his sword the brave
man draws. And asks no omen but
his country's cause.'"

Stone.

"Captain, Co. G. Residence or assignment, Portsmouth Date of Commission, Sept. 18, 1862. Mustered out June 21, 1865."

Adjutant General's Records, N. H.

Tredick, John H.—3rd N. H.

"Lieut. of Co. D [See below], 3rd N. H. Regt. Died at Fortress Monroe. . . Son of William and Mehitable Tredick."

"'Died for his Country,' Oh! do not deplore him:
His life was triumphal, his death was sublime.
His warfare complete, he has pass'd thro' the portal
That leads the freed soul to a glorified clime."

Stone.

"Corporal, Co. D. Residence, Portsmouth. Date of Muster, Aug. 23, 1861, for 3 years. Promoted to Sergeant, Aug. 8, 1862. Promoted to 1st Sergeant, March 8, 1863. Promoted to 2nd Lieutenant, Co. E. Commissioned Jan. 2, 1864. Wounded severely at Weir Bottom Church, Va., June 16, 1864. Died of wounds, July 6, 1864."

Adjutant General's Records, N. H.

Tucker, Charles H.—27th Maine.

"Corporal, Co. B. Born in Eliot, Maine. Resident of South Berwick, Maine. Date of Muster, Sept. 30, 1862, for 9 months. Mustered out and honorably discharged July 17, 1863, at Portland, Maine, by reason of expiration of term of service."

Adjutant General's Records, Maine.

Tucker, Henry—U. S. Navy.

Tucker, John A.—3rd N. H.

Member Storer Post, G. A. R.

"Corporal, Co. D. Residence or assignment, Greenland. Date of Muster, Aug. 23, 1861, for 3 years. Reduced to Private, Feb. 22, 1862. Wounded, Secessionville, S. C., June 16, 1862. Reënlisted Feb. 15, 1864. Private, Co. D. Residence or assignment, Portsmouth. Date of Muster, Feb. 15, 1864, for 3 years. Appointed Wagoner, May 20, 1864. Mustered out July 20, 1865."

Adjutant General's Records, N. H.

"Birthplace, Kingston, N. H. Received grape shot wound in left ankle at James Island, S. C., July [June] 16, 1862."

Post Records.

Tucker, Mark W.—16th N. H.

"Died at New Orleans." *Stone.*

"Private, Co. K. Residence or assignment, Portsmouth. Date of Muster, Oct. 28, 1862, for 9 months. Died of disease at Carrollton, La., Feb. 8, 1863."

Adjutant General's Records, N. H.

Tufts, John P.—40th N. Y.

Enlisted as "John P. Tufts."
"J. P. Tuffs." *Stone.*

"Private, Co. H. Enlisted June 17, 1861, for 3 years. Discharged Dec. 9, 1862, near Falmouth, Va., for disability."

Adjutant General's Records, N. Y.

Upham, Joseph B. Jr.—U. S. Navy.

Joseph Badger Upham, Jr.

"Born Dec. 25, 1840. Died Aug. 14, 1889. A good son. A loyal friend."

Stone.

"Third Assistant Engineer, 18 November, 1862. Second Assistant Engineer, 23 March, 1864. First Assistant Engineer, 1 January, 1868 [Title changed to Passed Assistant Engineer, by act of Congress approved 24 February, 1874]. Retired list, 27 December, 1875."

Hamersly's General Navy Register.

"Died at Portsmouth, N. H., August 13 [See above], 1889."

Navy Register, 1890.

Upham, Timothy—War 1812.

"Timothy Upham,
Born in Deerfield, N. H.,
September 9, 1783.
Died in Charlestown, Mass.,
November 2, 1855.
He was Lieut. Colonel, U. S. A.,
during the war of 1812,
and for many years
Collector of this Port."

Stone.

"Commissioned Major, 11th U. S. Infantry, March 12, 1812; and Lieutenant-Colonel, 21st U. S. Infantry, March 12, 1813."

Hamersly's Regular Army Register.

"Timothy Upham was of Portsmouth. He was the son of Rev. Timothy Upham, of Deerfield, where he was born in the year 1783. His mother was Hannah, the daughter of Rev. Nathaniel Gookin, of North Hampton. Timothy Upham moved to Portsmouth in 1807, and opened a store in Market street. In June, 1811, he was appointed, by Governor Langdon, one of his aids, with rank of Lieutenant-Colonel. He continued in business as a merchant until 1812, when, in anticipation of a war with Great Britain, he was commissioned a Major in the United States service in March of that year. In June following he was appointed to command the detachment of troops from New Hampshire ordered to garrison Fort McClary [in Portsmouth harbor], by Governor Plumer.

In July he was commissioned as Major of the 11th U. S. Infantry. In September he joined his regiment at Plattsburg, N. Y. January 15, 1813, he was ordered to Portland as superintendent of the recruiting district of Maine. In the spring he joined his regiment, and was detailed to command a battalion which was to join Gen. Hampton's army preparing to attack Montreal. On this futile expedition, Major (now Lieutenant-Colonel) Upham fought his battalion with credit at Crysler's Field. Just before this expedition he had been promoted to the Lieutenant-Coloneley of the 21st Regiment. On the 11th of September, 1814, he was in command of his regiment, at the 'sortie of Fort Erie,' and did gallant service with his regiment, in going to the rescue, by special order of Gen. Brown, of its former gallant commander, General Miller. At the close of this campaign, with impaired health, Col. Upham was ordered upon recruiting service.

At the close of the war he resigned his commission, and in 1816 was appointed Collector of Customs at Portsmouth, and continued in that office for thirteen years. In 1819, May 15, he was appointed Brigadier General of the 1st Brigade, 1st Division New Hampshire Militia, and was promoted to Major General of the Division May 19, 1820, upon the resignation of General Clement Storer. This office he resigned May 13, 1823.

After leaving the Custom-House in 1829, he again entered upon commercial pursuits, and in 1841 was appointed Navy Agent at Portsmouth by President Harrison. He soon resigned this office, and in 1845 removed to Charlestown, Mass., following his business of a merchant in Boston. Here his success did not meet his anticipations, and, impaired in health, he retired from active business. He died at Charlestown, November 2, 1855, in the 72d year of his age."

Adjutant General's Report, N. H., 1868.

Varney, Charles L.—U. S. Navy.

Waldren, Samuel W.—16th N. H.

"Died at Jackson Hospital, Memphis, Tenn., Aug. 24, 1863." *Stone.*

"Private, Co. E Residence or assignment, Portsmouth. Date of Muster, Oct. 25, 1862, for 9 months. Transferred to Co. K, Nov. 22, 1862. Discharged to date Aug. 20, 1863. Died at Memphis, Tenn., Aug. 23, 1863 [See above]."

Adjutant General's Records, N. H.

Waldron, N. S.—Mex. War.

"Second Lieutenant, U. S. Marine Corps, 13 September, 1831. First Lieutenant, 25 July, 1831. Captain, 16 March, 1847. Brevet Major, 22 July, 1848. Died 21 February, 1857."

Hamersly's General Navy Register.

Waldron, Samuel W. Jr.—31st N. Y. & U. S. Vols.

"Samuel Wallis Waldron. . . . President of the Common Council of Boston, Mass., in 1859. Lieutenant, Aide-de-Camp, Captain and Assistant Adjt. General in the war of the Rebellion."

Stone.

"Chaplain, 31st N. Y. Enrolled May 24, 1861, to serve 2 years. Mustered into service. Transferred Oct. 30, 1861, to Co. G, for appointment as 1st Lieutenant. Detailed as Aide-de Camp on General Newton's staff from Nov. 1st, 1861, to date of resignation. Discharged July 20, 1862, on tender of resignation."

Adjutant General's Records, N. Y.

"Appointed Captain, Asst. Adjutant General, of Volunteers, 14 July, 1862, from New York. Resigned 30 July, 1863."

Hamersly's Regular Army Register.

Walker, Wm. Augustus—27th Mass.

"Fell in battle near Richmond, Va. . . . He sleeps in southern soil." *Stone.*

"Captain. Co. C. Residence. Greenfield, Mass. Date of Muster, Sept. 10, 1861, for 3 years. Promoted to Major, May 29, 1863. Killed in action, June 3, 1864."
Adjutant General's Records, Mass.

Killed in battle at Cold Harbor, Va.

Wallace, Joseph—U. S. Navy.

Walsh, James—U. S. Navy.

Walsh, Richard—10th N. H. & U. S. Navy.

Enlisted as "Richard Welch."

"Son of David and Mary Walsh. Died July 17, 1864." *Stone.*

"Private, Co. G, 10th N. H. Residence, Portsmouth. Date of Muster, Sept. 12, 1862, for 3 years. Transferred to U. S. Navy, May 1, 1864. Died at Portsmouth, Va., Aug. 1, 1864 [See above]."
Adjutant General's Records, N. H.

Warburton, William—13th N. H.

"Private, Co. K Residence or assignment, Portsmouth. Date of Muster, Sept. 20, 1862, for 3 years. Discharged for disability at Portsmouth, Va., Jan. 22, 1864."
Adjutant General's Records, N. H.

Watkins, Benjamin F.—16th N. H.

"Died at New Orleans [See below]." *Stone.*

"Private, Co. K. Residence or assignment, Portsmouth. Date of Muster, Oct. 28, 1862, for 9 months. Died of disease at Carrollton, La., Feb. 4, 1863."
Adjutant General's Records, N. H.

Watkins, Daniel W.—16th N. H.

Enlisted as "Daniel Watkins."

"Died Sept. 13, 1863. . . . He sleeps in southern soil." *Stone.*

"Private, Co. K. Residence or assignment, Portsmouth. Date of Muster, Nov. 3, 1862, for 9 months. Died of disease at Memphis, Tenn., Aug. 13, 1863 [See above]."
Adjutant General's Records, N. H.

Webster, Henry C.—U. S. Navy.

"Act'g Master, U. S. N. [See below] died in Hospital at Plymouth, N. C., Sept. 23, 1862." *Stone.*

"Mate, 19 September, 1861. Died 19 September [See above] 1862".
Hamersly's General Navy Register.

Webster, Mark R.—War 1812.

Whaley, William Henry—10th & 2nd N. H.

Enlisted as "John Simpson."

"Private, Co. I, 10th N. H. Recruit. Residence or assignment, Plaistow. Date of Muster, August 11, 1863, for 3 years. Promoted to Corporal. Wounded slightly at Chapin's Farm, Va., Sept. 29, 1864. Appointed Sergeant, April 9, 1865. Transferred to 2nd N. H. V., June 21 1865.

Private, Co. D, 2nd N. H. Recruit. Residence or assignment, Plaistow. Date of Muster, August 11, 1863, for 3 years. Transferred from Co. I, 10th N. H. V., June 21, 1865. Mustered out December 19, 1865."
Adjutant General's Records, N. H.

Whidden, Andrew W.—10th N. H.

"Son of J. W. and E. R. Whidden. . . . Died in a rebel prison at Salisbury, N. C., Jan. 27, 1865, aged 20 years. His body lies not here.—There is rest in heaven for the weary and suffering soldiers." *Stone.*

"Private, Co. G. Residence, Portsmouth. Date of Muster, Sept. 4, 1862, for 3 years. Captured at Fair Oaks, Va., Oct. 27, 1864. Died at Salisbury, N. C., Feb. 17, 1865 [See above]."
Adjutant General's Records, N. H.

Whipple, Amiel W.—U. S. Army.

Amiel Weeks Whipple.

"Maj. Gen. A. W. Whipple,
3d Div., 3d Army Corps.
Major, Corps of
Engineers, U. S. Army—
Died of wounds received at the
battle of Chancellorsville, Va.,
May 7th, 1863,
Aged 45 years."
Stone.

"Born in Massachusetts. Appointed a Cadet at the U. S. Military Academy, from Massachusetts, in 1837. Graduated."

"2nd Lieut. 1st Artillery, 1 July, 1841. Transferred to Topographical Engineers, 28 Sept., 1841. 1st Lieut., 24 April, 1851. Captain, 1 July, 1855. Major, 9 Sept., 1861. Transferred to Engineers, 3 March, 1863. Died 7 May, 1863, of wounds received at the battle of Chancellorsville, Va. [4 May, 1863].

Brevet Rank:—Brevet Lieut. Colonel. 21 July, 1861, for gallant and meritorious service in the Manassas campaign. Brevet Colonel, 13 Dec., 1862, for gallant and meritorious service in the battle of Fredericksburg, Va. Brevet Brigadier General, 4 May, 1863, for gallant and meritorious service at the battle of Chancellorsville, where he was mortally wounded. Brevet Major General, 7 May, 1863, for gallant and meritorious service during the war."

"Appointed Brigadier General of Volunteers, 14 April, 1862. Major General of Volunteers, 3 May, 1863."

Hamersly's Regular Army Register.

"Whipple, Amiel Weeks, soldier, born in Greenwich, Mass., in 1818; died in Washington, D. C., 7 May, 1863. He studied at Amherst, was graduated at the U. S. Military Academy in 1841, was engaged immediately afterward in the hydrographic survey of Patapsco river, and in 1842 in surveying the approaches to New Orleans and the harbor of Portsmouth, N. H. In 1844 he was detailed as assistant astronomer upon the northeastern boundary survey, and in 1845 he was employed in determining the northern boundaries of New York, Vermont and New Hampshire. In 1849 he was appointed assistant astronomer in the Mexican boundary commission, and in 1853 he had charge of the Pacific railroad survey along the 35th parallel. In 1856 he was appointed engineer for the southern light-house district and superintendent of the improvements of St. Clair flats and St. Mary's river.

At the opening of the civil war he at once applied for service in the field, and was assigned as Chief Topographical Engineer on the staff of Gen. Irvin McDowell. In this capacity he was the author of the first maps of that part of Virginia that were issued during the war, and performed creditable service at the first battle of Fredericksburg.

Upon the second advance of the army he was attached, as Chief Topographical Engineer, to the staff of Gen. George B. McClellan, but, being appointed Brigadier-General of Volunteers, was recalled in May, 1862, and assigned to the command of the defences of Washington south of Potomac river. His service here was so well performed that he received in orders the thanks of the President of the United States.

His division was assigned in October, 1862, to the 9th corps, and took part in the movement down the eastern base of the Blue Ridge, upon the skirts of Lee's retreating army. At Waterloo his division was attached to the 3rd army corps, and he led it at the battle of Fredericksburg.

At the battle of Chancellorsville it was much exposed, and suffered more, probably, in that engagement than any other division of the army. He was shot on Monday, 4 May, 1863, when the battle was practically at an end, and, living three days, was appointed Major-General of Volunteers for gallantry in action. He had received the brevets of Lieutenant-Colonel for the Manassas campaign, Colonel for Fredericksburg, Brigadier General for Chancellorsville, and Major-General for services during the war—all in the regular army."

Appleton's Cyclopædia of American Biography.

Whipple, Prince—Rev. War.

His name appears on "Gen. Whipple's Staff Roll" for the Saratoga campaign in 1777, and the Rhode Island campaign in 1778.

"Prince Whipple [who is said to have been the son of an African prince] was a slave of General Whipple, but had his freedom from his master on condition of his good fighting."

When General Whipple started for Saratoga, "Prince was ordered to get the horses ready for the march. He was dilatory, and General Whipple upbraiding him, he replied thus: 'Master, you are going to fight for your liberty, but I have none to fight for.' 'Prince,' said the General, 'Behave like a man, and do your duty, and from this hour you shall be free.' Prince did his duty, accompanied his master in his expedition and was a freeman. — 'Brewster's Rambles about Portsmouth.'"

Adjutant General's Report, N. H., Vol. 2, 1866.

"Prince Whipple died in this town [Portsmouth] in 1797, twelve years after his former master. He was a large, well-proportioned and fine looking man, and of gentlemanly manners and deportment."

Rambles About Portsmouth, First Series.

The grave of Prince Whipple in the North Cemetery, Portsmouth, was identified a few years since by his grandson, John Smith. It is in the southern part of the cemetery, south-west from General Whipple's stone, and next east of the foot stone of Capt. Theodore Furber, but is unmarked except by two rough stones which scarcely appear above the surface of the ground.

Whipple, William—Rev. War.

"Here are deposited the remains
Of the Honorable William Whipple
who departed this Life
on the 28th day of November, 1785,
in the 55th year of his Age.

He was often elected
and thrice attended
the Continental Congress
as Delegate
for the State of New Hampshire,
particularly in that memorable year
in which
America declared itself independent
of Great Britain.
He was also at the Time of his decease
a Judge
of the supreme Court of Judicature.
In Him
a firm & ardent Patriotism
was united with
universal benevolence
and every social Virtue."

Stone.

"Whipple, William, signer of the Declaration of Independence, born in Kittery, Maine, 14 January, 1730; died in Portsmouth, N. H., 28 November, 1785. His father, William, a native of Ipswich, Mass., was bred as a malster, but, removing to Kittery, engaged in a seafaring life for several years. The son was educated at a public school in his native town, and afterward became a sailor, having command of a vessel before he was twenty-one years of age. He engaged in the European, West India, and African trade, and brought large numbers of negro slaves to this country, but afterward, during the Revolution, liberated those that belonged to him. In 1759 he abandoned the sea entirely and entered into business in Portsmouth with his brother Joseph, which connection lasted till about two years previous to the Revolution.

At an early period of the contest between the colonies and Great Britain he took a decided part in favor of the former. He was elected a delegate from New Hampshire to the Continental Congress in 1775, taking his seat in May, was re-elected, 23 January, 1776, took his seat on 29 February following, and signed the Declaration of Independence in July. He was re-elected to Congress in 1778, and declined to be chosen again, but was a member of the state assembly in 1780-4. He was commissioned a Brigadier General in 1777, commanded a brigade of New Hampshire troops at the battles of Saratoga and Stillwater, and, after the surrender of Burgoyne, signed the articles of capitulation with Col. James Wilkinson on behalf of General Horatio Gates. General Whipple was afterward selected as one of the officers under whose charge the British troops were conducted to their place of encampment on Winter Hill, near Boston. In 1778, he participated in General Sullivan's expedition to Rhode Island, and he resigned his military appointment, 20 June, 1782. In 1780 he was appointed a commissioner of the board of admiralty, which post he declined. He was state superintendent of finances in 1782-4, appointed judge of the supreme court 20 June, 1782, and justice of the peace and quorum throughout the s ate in December, 1784 and acted in this capacity till his death."

Appleton's Cyclopedia of American Biography.

The Whipple School in Portsmouth, was thus named in 1890, in honor of William Whipple, Signer of the Declaration of Independence, by the city of Portsmouth, at the suggestion of Storer Post, G. A. R.; which, in the following year presented an oil portrait of General Whipple to the city, to be placed in the school, where it may now be seen.

Additional information in relation to General Whipple will be found in the Appendix to "The Presentation of Flags to the Schools of Portsmouth, N. H., October 9th, 1890, by Storer Post," Portsmouth, 1890; and in "The Presentation of the Portraits of General William Whipple and Admiral David Glasgow Farragut, November 20th, 1891, by Storer Post to the city of Portsmouth, N. H." Portsmouth, 1891. The Farragut portrait was presented for, and has been placed at the Farragut school, which name, at the request of the Board of Mayor and Aldermen of Portsmouth, was also suggested by Storer Post.

White, John—7th N. H.

"Private, Co. G. Residence or assignment, Manchester. Date of Muster, Nov. 28, 1861, for 3 years. Wounded slightly at Fort Wagner, S. C., July 18, 1863. Rëenlisted, Private, Co. G. Residence or assignment, Portsmouth. Date of Muster, Feb. 28, 1864, for 3 years. Wounded near Laurel Hill, Va., Oct. 7, 1864. Mustered out July 20, 1865."

Adjutant General's Records, N. H.

Whitehouse, Eben E.—War 1812.

Whitehouse, Samuel N.—U. S. Navy.

"Carpenter, U. S. Navy, from 1861 to the time of his death." *Stone.*

"Carpenter, 17 July, 1861."

Hamersly's General Navy Register.

"Retired list, March 8, 1890."—"Died at Brooklyn, N. Y., January 2, 1891."

Navy Registers, 1891 and 1892.

Whittier, Samuel C.—11th & 23rd Mass.

Member Storer Post, G. A. R.

"Assistant Surgeon, 11th Mass. Residence, Boston. Date of Commission, August 29, 1862.

Surgeon, 23rd Mass. Date of Commission, May 26, 1864 Mustered out June 25, 1865."

Adjutant General's Records, Mass.

"Birthplace, Dover, N. H."

Post Records.

Samuel C. Whittier, M. D., died in Portsmouth, N. H., February 1st, 1893.

"Samuel Crook Whittier was born at Dover, this state, Jan. 3, 1837, and was, consequently, 56 years old at the time of his death. He was the third son of John and Hannah (Hanson) Whittier, a grandson of Obadiah, and a cousin to the poet John Greenleaf Whittier.

He attended school at West Lebanon, Me., and was fitted for college at Franklin Academy, Dover.

He graduated from Harvard Medical College in the summer of 1862, and on the 29th of August, of the same year, was commissioned Assistant Surgeon of the 11th Mass. Vol. Infantry, which regiment he joined at Fairfax Seminary, Va., on the 4th of September following.

He remained with this regiment, rendering his country distinguished services, until May 26, 1864, when he was commissioned Surgeon of the 23d Mass. Vol. Infantry, with which organization he remained until his muster out in June, 1865. Both commissions bear the autograph of Massachusetts' celebrated war governor, John A. Andrew.

At the battle of Gettysburg, Surgeon Whittier was placed in charge of a large number of wounded Confederate officers, captured in Pickett's memorable charge, and it was to him the dying Mississippian, Gen. Barksdale, said: 'Why was Hooker succeeded by Meade? We will whip you tomorrow.'

Returning from the war he practised medicine and surgery for a time in Lynn and Boston, Mass., and in Great Falls, this state."

"On the 22d of November, 1869, Dr. Whittier took up his residence in this city, where he has since lived." "As a physician and surgeon he took high rank," and "every one of his patients considered him a friend as well as physician."

He was a member of "Storer Post, No. 1, Grand Army of the Republic, in which he was mustered May 26, 1884, and had held for several years the position of Surgeon.

On the Sunday preceeding Memorial Day, 1891, at the service held by Storer Post in Grand Army hall in commemoration of its comrades who had died during the preceding year, Dr. Whittier delivered the Memorial address, pronounced by those who heard it one of the most eloquent, impressive and tenderly pathetic efforts ever delivered in Grand Army hall on a similar occasion."

Portsmouth Daily Eve. Times, Feb. 1, 1893.

"The funeral services over the remains of Dr. S. C. Whittier were held at the Middle street Baptist church, Sunday [Feb. 5, 1893], Rev. H. M. Dean officiating, Rev. Wm. H. Alden, D. D., being unable to come. The church was filled with the friends of the deceased and large delegations from Osgood Lodge, I. O. O F., De Witt Clinton Commandery, Knights Templar, and Storer Post, G. A. R Both of the impressive services of the Odd Fellows and Knights Templar were performed in the church, and those of the Grand Army at the cemetery."

Portsmouth Daily Eve. Post, Feb. 6, 1893.

Wholley, James—30th Mass.

Member Storer Post, G. A. R.

"James Wholey." *Stone.*

"Private, Co. E Residence, Lawrence, Mass. Enlisted Oct. 29, 1861. Date of Muster, Oct. 29, 1861, for 3 years. Mustered out Nov. 29, 1864."

Adjutant General's Records, Mass.

Wiggin, Samuel P.—War 1812.

Willey, Henry J.—10th N. H.

Enlisted as "Henry I. Willey."

"H. J. W." *Stone.*

"Private, Co. G. Residence or assignment, Portsmouth. Date of Muster, Sept. 4, 1862, for 3 years. Promoted to Corporal. Reduced to Private at his own request, Oct., 1862. Promoted to Corporal, Dec. 21, 1864. Promoted to Sergeant, Feb. 1, 1865. Mustered out June 21, 1865."

Adjutant General's Records, N. H.

Willey, John—War 1812.

"Capt. John Willey died at Faith Home [Portsmouth, N. H.]. . . . A veteran of the war of 1812." *Stone.*

Wilson, Robert—U. S. Navy.

Wingate, William—10th N. H.

"Private, Co. G. Residence or assignment, Portsmouth. Date of Muster, Sept. 4, 1862, for 3 years. Mustered out June 21, 1865."

Adjutant General's Records, N. H.

Wood, Charles A.—U. S. M. C.

His stone reads incorrectly—"C. A. Wood, U. S. Navy."

Yates, Arthur R.—U. S. Navy.

Member Storer Post, G. A. R.

"Arthur Reid Yates, Captain, U. S. N. 1838-1891." *Stone.*

"Acting Midshipman, 24 September. 1856 [1853]. Midshipman, 10 June, 1857. Passed Midshipman, 25 June, 1860. Master, 24 October, 1860. Lieutenant, 18 April, 1861. Lieutenant-Commander. 16 November, 1864. Commander, 6 February, 1872."

Hamersly's General Navy Register.

"Appointed from New York. . . Captain, 9 February, 1884."

Navy Register, 1891.

"Born in New York. Entered Naval Academy, September 24, 1853; graduated. 1857: from 1857 until 1860, in steamer 'Mississippi', Asiatic squadron; July 1860, until December, 1860, in steam-sloop 'Brooklyn', Gulf Squadron; from December. 1860, until December, 1863, in the sloop 'Cyane', Pacific Squadron.

Commissioned as Lieutenant, April 18, 1861; from January, 1864, until August, 1864, steamer 'Augusta'; a volunteer on board the flag-ship 'Hartford' at battle of Mobile Bay (See Admiral Farragut's Report): evening of day of the battle, placed in command of the captured gunboat 'Selma'; from that time until June, 1867, successively in command of 'Selma', 'J. P. Jackson', and 'Chocura', Gulf Squadron.

Commissioned as Lieutenant-Commander, November 16, 1864; September, 1867, until June, 1868, Executive-Officer of flag-ship 'Piscataqua', Asiatic Squadron; from June. 1868 until July, 1869, successively in command of steamers 'Ashuelot' and 'Unadilla', same Squadron: Naval Academy, 1870-2.

Commissioned as Commander, February 6, 1872: commanding 'Manhattan' (iron-clad), North Atlantic Station. 1873: commanding receiving-ship 'Sabine' [Portsmouth, N. H.,] 1875-6; League Island Navy Yard, 1877-8; commanding 'Alliance', North Atlantic Station, 1879-81; Navy Yard, Portsmouth, 1881-4.

Promoted to Captain. February, 1884; commanding training-ship 'New Hampshire', 1884-7; waiting orders, 1887-8: commanding 'Pensacola', Asiatic [North Atlantic] Station, 1888-90."

Hamersly's Naval Records, 1890.

"Birthplace, Schenectady, New York; residence, Portsmouth, N. H. . . . Captain of Yard, Navy Yard, Portsmouth, N. H., 1890-1.

Died at U. S. Navy Yard, Portsmouth, November 4, 1891."

Soldiers Memorial, 1892.

"A resolution tendering the thanks of Congress to Vice-Admiral David G. Farragut. and to the officers, petty officers, seamen, and marines under his command. for their gallantry and good conduct in the action in Mobile Bay on the 5th August, 1864.

That the thanks of Congress are eminently due, and are hereby tendered, to Vice-Admiral David G. Farragut, of the United States Navy, and to the officers, petty officers, seamen, and marines under his command, for the unsurpassed gallantry and skill exhibited by them in the engagement in Mobile Bay on the 5th day of August. 1864, and for their long and faithful services and unwavering devotion to the cause of the country in the midst of the greatest difficulties and dangers.

Sec. 2. That the President of the United States be requested to communicate this resolution to Vice-Admiral Farragut, and that the Secretary of the Navy be requested to communicate the same to the officers, seamen, and marines of the Navy by general order of his department.

Approved February 10, 1866."

Hamersly's General Navy Register.

Captain Arthur R. Yates delivered an eloquent address on the presentation of a U. S. flag, by Storer Post, in 1890, to the Farragut School, which will be found in "The Presentation of Flags to the Schools of Portsmouth, N. H , October 9th, 1890, by Storer Post," Portsmouth, 1890. His death was deeply lamented by many friends.

Yeaton, John B.—1st U. S. Art.

Young, Charles E.—1st N. H. H. Art.

"Private, Co. A. Residence or assignment, Portsmouth. Date of Muster, July 18, 1863, for three years. Discharged for disability at Fort Sumner, D. C., Dec. 15, 1864."

Adjutant General's Records, N. H.

Young, George B.—44th Mass.

"Son of Elijah and Mary H. Young. Died at Newbern, N. C., Feb. 2, 1863."

Stone.

"Private, Co. G. Residence, Andover, Mass. Enlisted———. Date of Muster, Sept. 12, 1862, for 9 months. Died at

Newbern, N. C., Feb. 3, 1863 [See above]."

Adjutant General's Records, Mass.

Young, Willard W.—26th Maine.

Member Storer Post, G. A. R.

"Storer Post, No. 1, G. A R."

Stone.

"Private, Co. C. Born in Trenton, Maine. Resident of Tremont, Maine. Date of Muster, Oct. 11, 1862, for 9 months. Mustered out and honorably discharged, Aug. 17, 1863, at Bangor, Maine, by reason of expiration of service."

Adjutant General's Records, Maine.

Young, William C.—Mex. War.

William Cutter Young.

ADDENDA.

REVOLUTIONARY WAR.

The following names were omitted from the alphabetical list of "The Graves We Decorate," as the burial place of Lieut. Elijah Hall could not be ascertained, although he is supposed to have been buried in the Episcopal Cemetery, adjoining St. John's Church, Portsmouth, and Rev. Samuel Langdon, D. D., is buried at Hampton Falls, N. H.

A tablet to the memory of the former has been placed in St. John's, and to the latter in the North Church, Portsmouth.

Hall, Elijah—Rev. War.

"In memory
of the
Hon. Elijah Hall,
who died
June 22, A. D. 1830,
aged 84 years.
As an Officer of the Ranger, under
Capt. J. Paul Jones; a Merchant; a
Representative, Senator and
Councillor of this State; as
Naval Officer; Member of this
Church, and in his other relations,
he sustained the character of a
Patriot and an upright Man."

Tablet, St. John's Church, Portsmouth.

"Died. In this town, on Tuesday last [June 22, 1830], Hon. Elijah Hall, aged 87 [See above]. Capt. Hall was Lieutenant in the Navy in the Revolutionary war, sailed under John Paul Jones in the 'Ranger;' was many years elected Counsellor from this district; and for several years prior to his death was Naval Officer of the District of Portsmouth.

He was, in private life, an estimable citizen, a fair merchant, a tender parent, and an honest man."

Portsmouth Journal, June 26, 1830.

"Lieut. Elijah Hall," a "brave and meritorious officer, . . . served with the Chevalier John Paul Jones," . . . and "was a lieutenant under the Chevalier in the 'Ranger.'

Lieut. Hall had entered on board this vessel at Portsmouth, N. H., before her departure for France [Nov. 1, 1777], and was in her with Jones in his cruise on the coasts of Scotland and Ireland, in the descent on Whitehaven, and in the battle with the 'Drake' [April 24, 1778]. When [Lieut]. Simpson behaved so badly as to disobey orders, it was Hall that was selected to arrest him, and to command the 'Drake' in his stead. The prominent traits of Lieut. Hall's character were promptitude and energy; of which he gave a remarkable instance in repairing the 'Drake' in the course of one night, with the assistance of forty men, after Simpson had pronounced it impossible in her then shattered condition.

Lieut. Hall went to Brest with Jones; and when, through the benevolence of the latter, Simpson was put in command of the 'Ranger' for the purpose of returning to America, Hall occupied the post of first lieutenant.

After his return to the United States, he was engaged in several expeditions against the enemy, on board the same ship, with Commodore Whipple, and was very successful in making captures, most of which arrived safely in port. When the 'America,' 74, was assigned to Jones, he offered Lieut. Hall a very honorable and efficient station in her; but the gift of that vessel to France frustrated his good intentions.

Lieut. Hall eventually proceeded in the 'Ranger,' with other ships of war, to assist in the defence of Charleston, S. C., where he fell into the hands of the enemy, in common with the garrison, by capitulation [May 11, 1780]. He returned to New Hampshire, but was not exchanged until a general surrender of prisoners. He never resigned his commission, and was always ready for active service.

At the close of the war of the Revolution he engaged in commercial pursuits, by which he enriched himself; but suffered considerably by the British orders in council, and the French Berlin and Milan decrees.

Although offered a pension by government, he would not receive it, but accepted the appointment of Naval Officer for Portsmouth, a situation which he still retains [1825], at the advanced age of 83 [See above]. With the snow of so many winters upon his head, he discharges his duty, it is understood, with the greatest satisfaction to the merchants and others, affording proof of an uncommon vigor of constitution and strength of intellect. Faithful to his country and true to his duty in every situation, there can be no doubt that a consciousness of probity has ensured for him that intellectual tranquillity which is so favorable to human life.

As far as the author of this work is informed, Commodore [Richard] Dale and Lieutenant Hall are [were in 1825] the only surviving officers of all those who, at various times, sailed with and fought under the Chevalier John Paul Jones. Time has laid others in the dust; but seems to have preserved these two venerable men as a sample of the stout hearts and strong frames of the heroes who braved the shores and squadrons of Great Britain, and plucked laurels in her very ports to deck the brow and promote the glory of infant America."

Sherburne's Life of John Paul Jones.

An interesting account of the cruise of the "Ranger," under John Paul Jones, will be found in the N. E. H. G. Register, Vol XXIX, pages 13 and 170.

Hon. Elijah Hall long resided and died in the house now Nos. 36 and 38 Daniel street, Portsmouth.

Langdon, Samuel—Rev. War.

"In Memoriam.
Rev. Samuel Langdon, D. D.
Born in Boston, Jan. 11, 1723.
Chaplain to the New Hampshire troops at the siege of Louisburg, in 1745.
Pastor of this Church, 1747 to 1774.
President of Harvard College, 1774 to 1780. Offered the prayer for the assembled army the night previous to the battle of Bunker Hill.
An influential member of the N. H. Constitutional Convention in 1788, for the adoption of the Federal Constitution.
Pastor of the Church at Hampton Falls, 1781 to 1797.
Died. Nov. 29, 1797."

Tablet, North Church, Portsmouth.

"In the auditorium of the North Congregational church in this city, near the entrance to the northern aisle, is a mural tablet, exquisitely wrought in statuary marble, spotless and pure as was the scholar, statesman, patriot, whose name it celebrates, erected by Mrs. Thomas Aston Harris of Portsmouth, N. H., in loving memory of her great-grandfather. Rev. Samuel Langdon, D. D."

"Dr. Langdon was a noted man of letters, and throughout his life was connected with and interested in educational matters, and while assistant pastor of the North church he taught the grammar school in Portsmouth up to the date of his departure for Louisburg. Afterward, during his full pastorate, he built the house in which Capt. and Mrs. Harris now reside, on Pleasant street, and occupied it during his pastoral connection with the church. The mansion has been in the possession of the family and occupied by them uninterruptedly since that period.

He graduated at Harvard in 1740, with high honors, his conspicuous merit afterward winning distinguished recognition by his elevation to the presidential chair of his college. In public affairs he naturally exercised a profound influence; this was felt in the Constitutional Convention of 1788, where, by his voice and example he contributed more perhaps, than any other man to the favorable action of that body."

Portsmouth Daily Eve. Times, Jan. 1, 1891.

"Landgon, Samuel, clergyman, born in Boston, Mass., 12 Jan. 1723 [See above]: died in Hampton Falls, N. H., 29 Nov., 1797.

He was graduated at Harvard in 1740, and while teaching in Portsmouth, N. H., studied theology, and was licensed to preach. In 1745 he was appointed Chaplain of a regiment, and was present at the capture of Louisburg.

On his return he was appointed assistant to Rev. James Fitch, of the North Church of Portsmouth, was ordained Pastor in 1747, and continued in that charge till 1774, when he became President of Harvard. His ardent patriotism led him to adopt measures that were obnoxious to the Tory students, and although he endeavored to administer the government of the college with justice, his resignation was virtually compelled in 1780. The next year he became pastor of the Congregational church at Hampton Falls, N. H.

In 1788 he was a delegate to the New Hampshire convention that adopted the Constitution of the United States, often led its debates, and did much to remove prejudice against the Constitution.

He was distinguished as a scholar and theologian, and exerted a wide influence in his community. The University of Aberdeen gave him the degree of D. D. in 1762, and he was a member of the

American academy of arts and sciences from its foundation. He published 'Summary of Christian Faith and Practice' (1768); 'Observations on the Revelations' (1791); 'Remarks on the Leading Sentiments of Dr. Hopkins' System of Doctrines' (1794); and many sermons. In 1761, in connection with Col. Joseph Blanchard, he prepared and published a map of New Hampshire."

Appleton's Cyclopædia of American Biography.

PRE-REVOLUTION.

The services of the following named men in the British Navy and in the Colonial Wars, while we were yet subjects of Great Britain, should cause their memory to be preserved.

Coues, Peter—British Navy.

"This Stone
Marks the Grave
of
Peter Coues
who died
Nov. 29, 1818.
Æt. 86"

Stone.—Pleasant St. Cemetery.—North east.

For date of birth and age see below.

"Among the venerable citizens of Portsmouth of half a century ago [1869], we well remember Capt. Peter Coues, a gentleman of independent circumstances, who might be seen, with his cane under his arm on State street, or in the vicinity. His residence previous to the fire of 1813, was on the southwest corner of Atkinson and State streets [the latter being then named Buck street], on the spot where W. J. Laighton's house now [1869] stands. In the old dwelling house was a store where for many years he kept ship chandlery, merchandise, groceries, etc.

In early life Capt. Peter Coues was pressed into the British service [See below]. He was at one time sailing-master of the famous 'Royal George,' which was afterwards, in 1782, sunk in the British Channel [Portsmouth harbor, England] with eight hundred men on board. He also served in the capacity of midshipman. After several years service in the British Navy, he returned to Portsmouth before the American Revolution, where, by that urbanity of mind and simplicity of manners for which seafaring men of liberal views are generally distinguished, he obtained a good standing among his fellow citizens, and died on the 29th of November, 1818, at the advanced age of eighty-three years [See below]."

Rambles About Portsmouth, Second Series.

Capt. Peter Coues was born in Portsmouth, July 30, 1736. He was the son of Peter Coues, senior, who was born in the Parish of Saint Peters in the Island of Jersey, in the English Channel, about the year 1710, settled in Portsmouth, and married Mary Long of this town, Nov. 4, 1735. Mary Long, probably born in Plymouth, England, was the daughter of Emanuel and Mary (Carne) Long, and grand-daughter of George and Ursula (Wills) Carne, of "Endellia" and "Plimton," near Plymouth, England.

As Commodore Digby Dent, R. N.—who was Commodore on the Jamaica Station in 1747, and a "Commissioner of the Navy" from 1756 to 1761 (See "Charnock's Biographia Navalis," London, 1796, Vol. IV, pages 378-380), served many years in the West Indies, when he perhaps visited Portsmouth—was his mother's cousin: Capt. Peter Coues was probably appointed a Midshipman in the British Navy, when a boy, through his influence, and the statement in the "Rambles," that he was "pressed," is doubtless an error. Another cousin, Captain Cotton Dent, R. N., also commanded a sloop-of-war on the Jamaica Station, in 1744 (See "Charnock," Vol. V, pages 440-1).

Family traditions relate that Capt. Coues took part in several battles, and was at one time sailing-master of the "Royal George."

The Dents have continued a Naval family, and Vice Admiral Charles Bayley Calmady Dent, R. N., retired,—great-great grandson of Captain Cotton Dent, R. N., brother of Commodore Digby Dent, R. N., both sons of Captain Digby Dent, R. N., and Ursula (Carne) Dent—is the seventh in a direct line, father and son, of British Admirals and Captains.

Captain Digby Dent, R. N., who married a sister of Mary (Carne) Long died a Commodore on the Jamaica Station August 19, 1737 (See "Charnock," Vol. IV, page 57).

Loss of the Royal George.

WILLIAM COWPER.

"The 'Royal George,' of 108 guns, while undergoing a partial careening in Portsmouth harbor [England], was overset about 10 a. m., August 29, 1782. The total loss was believed to be near one thousand souls."

"Toll for the brave!
The brave that are no more!
All sunk beneath the wave,
Fast by their native shore!

Eight hundred of the brave,
Whose courage well was tried,
Had made the vessel heel,
And laid her on her side.

A land-breeze shook the shrouds,
And she was overset;
Down went the Royal George,
With all her crew complete.

Toll for the brave!
Brave Kempenfelt is gone;
His last sea-fight is fought,
His work of glory done.

It was not in the battle;
No tempest gave the shock:
She sprang no fatal leak,
She ran upon no rock.

His sword was in its sheath,
His fingers held the pen,
When Kempenfelt went down
With twice four hundred men.

Weigh the vessel up
Once dreaded by our foes!
And mingle with our cup
The tear that England owes.

Her timbers yet are sound,
And she may float again,
Full charged with England's thunder,
And plough the distant main:

But Kempen'elt is gone,
His victories are o'er;
And he and his eight hundred
Shall plough the wave no more."

Harper's Cyclopedia of British and American Poetry.

Hale, Samuel—Colonial War.

"Samuel Hale, Esquire, A. A. S.
Died July 10th, A D., 1807,
Aged 89.
Fix'd in correct Religious & Moral habits he exhibited to the World the efficacy of a virtuous life, and in his death the holy triumphs of a Christian."

Stone.—North Cemetery—Center.

"Samuel Hale was born in Newbury, Mass., in 1718, and graduated at Harvard College in 1740. He removed to Portsmouth soon after, and became a teacher. He engaged in the Louisburg expedition as a Captain in Col. Moore's Regiment, and was made Major of the same, Oct. 7, 1745. After his return he became the instructor of the Latin grammar school in Portsmouth, and continued as such for near forty years, distinguished for discipline and aptness as a teacher. For his services he was rewarded by the grant of the town of Weare, which for a long time was known as Halestown. He was Representative and Judge of the Court of Common Pleas for Rockingham, and died July 7, 1807, in the 89th year of his age."

Adjutant General's Report, N. H, Vol. 2, 1866.

Hart, John—Colonial War.

"In Peace
Amidst ye Rage of Noise & War,
Here Rests the Remains
of Col. John Hart, Esqr.
who departed this Life
Octo. 30th, 1777.
Aged 72 Years."

Stone.—North Cemetery.—North-east.

"Col. John Hart was of a prominent family of Portsmouth. He was Captain of a company in Col. Meserve's regiment of 1756, and Lieutenant-Colonel of the same, which regiment was attached to the expedition against Crown Point."

"In 1758 New Hampshire raised still another regiment for 'the Crown Point Expedition' This numbered eight hundred men, and was commanded by Col. John Hart, of Portsmouth. A portion of the regiment [under Col. Hart] was ordered to join the expedition against Louisburg, and the remainder did duty under Lieut. Col. Goffe on the western frontier."

Adjutant General's Report, N. H., Vol. 2, 1866.

"Col. John Hart was the owner of the land now used as the North burying-ground, and it did not become town property until 1753, little more than a century [140 years] ago, when Col. Hart sold it to the town for £150, on condition that it should be kept for a burying-ground."

Rambles About Portsmouth, First Series.

www.ingramcontent.com/pod-product-compliance
Lightning Source LLC
Chambersburg PA
CBHW021526270326
41930CB00008B/1108

* 9 7 8 3 3 3 7 3 1 8 2 2 2 *